Market, Bureaucracy and Community

Market, Bureaucracy and Community

A Student's Guide to Organisation

Hal Colebatch and Peter Larmour

Pluto  Press

LONDON · BOULDER, COLORADO

First published 1993 by Pluto Press
345 Archway Road, London N6 5AA, UK
and 5500 Central Avenue
Boulder, Colorado 80301, USA

British Library Cataloguing in Publication Data
A catalogue record for this book is available from the British Library

ISBN 0 7453 0762 0 hb
ISBN 0 7453 0763 9 pb

Library of Congress Cataloging in Publication Data
Colebatch, H. K. (Hal K.)
    Market, bureaucracy and community: a student's guide to
organisation / by Hal Colebatch and Peter Larmour.
       p.   cm.
    Includes bibliographical references and index.
    ISBN 0-7453-0762-0. –ISBN 0-7453-0763-9 (pbk.)
    1. Organization–Case studies. I. Larmour, Peter. II. Title.
HD31.C6113 1994
302.3'5–dc20   93-33091
                                                                         CIP

Designed and Produced for Pluto Press by
Chase Production Services, Chipping Norton
Typeset from authors' disk by
Stanford DTP Services, Milton Keynes
Printed in the EC by T.J. Press, Padstow

Contents

Preface

This book is a guide for students who want to analyse, compare and understand organisation in the public, private or voluntary sectors. It is written for people coming to the subject for the first time, whether in their final years of secondary schooling, as undergraduates, as trainees, or in professionally-oriented postgraduate courses.

People are questioning existing forms of organisation and demanding that they change, for example by becoming more responsive, or more entrepreneurial. Others are defending them, for example against cutbacks. On a small scale, for example, there are debates about whether children with disabilities should be cared for in large institutions or by families. Meanwhile, governments are contracting out services formerly provided by big hospitals, and what counts as a family is being contested. On a large scale there are debates about whether governments should do more, or less, to promote economic growth. Governments in many countries are privatising public utilities, while the collapse of the socialist states raises urgent questions about the role of the government in the development of a market economy. We hope that students who read this book will better understand the organisational context of their own lives, and be better able to propose and criticise new organisational arrangements.

Organisation is studied within a number of academic disciplines and for different professional purposes: the book aims to be an introduction suitable for people in a range of fields. We have tried to provide a readily understood introduction rather than a survey or critique of the academic literature on organisations. We come to the subject with backgrounds in political science but find ourselves crossing established disciplinary boundaries. Our approach reflects our interests in so-called 'rational choice' and 'interpretist' theories of organisation and our experience in teaching undergraduates. Other approaches are possible.

The book develops three models of organisation, here called 'community', 'the market' and 'bureaucracy', which are pervasive in the social sciences. These models are then applied to cases chosen to illuminate their characteristics, and the relationships between them: youth homelessness, the epidemic of HIV/AIDS and broadcasting. The cases have been written to apply generally to industrial countries (other cases could be developed applying the approach to developing countries). The models are then used to consider issues of power, change and evaluation in organisation.

To make points about organisation, we refer to experiences common to students, but we recognise that these may be specific to Australia. To keep it readable, there is a minimum of references within the text, but a list of suggestions for further reading concludes each chapter, and there is a glossary of key words at the end of the book.

Further Reading

For more advanced texts that adopt related approaches see Harmon and Mayer (1986), Hood (1986), and (for Britain) Marchment and Thompson eds (1993), and the related set of readings for an Open University course, Thompson et al eds (1991). For issues in teaching the University of Tasmania course, see Colebatch and Larmour (1991).

For texts about organisation from disciplinary points of view see: for management, Dunford (1992) and Mintzberg (1973); for political science and public administration, Self (1977) and Dunleavy (1991); for sociology, Clegg (1989, 1990) and Morgan (1986); and for economics Williamson (1985) and Hodgson (1988).

For examples of recent accounts of changing organisational arrangements, see Denhardt (1993) on new public managers in Australia, the USA, Canada and Britain; Peters (1992) on 'necessary disorganisation'; Osborne and Gaebler (1993) on 'reinventing government' in the USA; Deakin and Wright (1990) on 'consuming public services' in Britain; or Hilmer (1989) on new forms of organising in Australia.

Acknowledgements

The book was developed from a first-year Administration course the authors taught at the University of Tasmania in 1990–91. We are very grateful for the tolerance, critical comments and positive suggestions we got from students and tutors involved in that course, and Dr Harry Stanton who helped evaluate it. We presented a paper on teaching the course, and benefited from the subsequent discussion in the 'academics and practitioners' group of the annual conference of the Royal Institute of Public Administration, Australia, held in Hobart in 1990.

Dennis Altman, John Ballard, Stephen Bell, Michael Brooks, Ralph Chapman, Andrew Dunsire, Geoff Fougere, Michael Harmon, Marcus Haward, Carol Healy, Nancy Larmour, Adrian Leftwich, John Power, Warren Talbot, Grahame Thompson, Ian Thynne, Liz Thynne, Nick Toonen, Malcolm Waters and two anonymous readers commented on earlier versions of the text, or parts of it, or helped find people who could. We hope it has improved as a result, but we remain responsible for the defects. We are very grateful to Rosemary Smuts who formated, improved the grammar and clarified the meaning of the semi-final version.

1 Introduction

This book is concerned with the analysis of organisation. Our primary focus is on organisation as such, rather than on the characteristics or the problems of particular organisations. We are concerned with the different patterns of organisation that we might find, and with what people do to bring these about.

We take what might be called an 'action perspective' on organisation; that is, we see organisation as something that people do. Certainly, there are things called 'organisations', but they are there because people act in a particular way. 'Organisation' is a way of describing this pattern of activity.

Not all organisations will have the same pattern: the pattern of activity in the army may be rather different from that found in an environmental protest group, and the pattern in a family-run corner store may be different from that of a large department store chain.

These differences in the pattern of activity come about partly because people draw on shared ideas about how to organise in particular contexts: what is seen as appropriate in the army may be seen as quite unacceptable in the environmental protest group.

There may be degrees of organisation. We see a group of children kicking a football around; we might look more closely to see just what is going on. Do they seem to be in two teams? Are there clear goals? Are the rules of football being enforced? Is there an umpire? Is anyone keeping the score? In other words, is the activity (kicking a football) an organised game?

Where organised activity is associated with written rules and legally constituted bodies it is often called 'formal organisation'. This term indicates the existence of recognised, labelled rules and roles: about the 'referee', for instance, or 'off-side'. It also implies that there can be 'informal organisation' – that is, people working together without any formal labels. Informal organisation may be an alternative to formal organisation (e.g. the child care arrangements that parents may make with relatives and neighbours). Or the informal organisation may be recognised within formal organisation – for instance, people may use networks of friends to find out what's going on at work. And formality is likely to be a matter of degree: not so much 'is this a formal organisation or not?' but 'to what extent is this a formal organisation? And what exactly makes it formal?'

In this perspective we can see formal organisation and informal organisation as complementary rather than polar opposites, which may be found together in varying combinations. Informal organisation, e.g. friendship and a shared love of the game, may be enough for an afternoon's football, but to organise a season, you need captains for the teams, a schedule of matches, guaranteed access to grounds, some way of publicising the arrangements and dealing with any uncertainties – in other words, formal organisation. As an organisation expands it is likely that it will rely more on formal processes. Similarly, the more an organisation has to relate to 'outside' bodies the more likely it is to have formal office-bearers, rules and procedures. But within this formal organisation, informal organisation may grow, e.g. the (formal) delegates from the clubs may develop (informal) ways of working together and even friendships, all of which facilitate the working of the (formal) organisational procedures.

We probably know already that there are different degrees of organisation. We might apply different sorts of test in making our judgements about how organised any particular example was, depending on the circumstances and our purposes. If we were running a local tennis competition and we received an application from the 'Cascades Tennis Club' to enter a team, we might want to know only the name and phone number of the secretary, and the names of the players. But if this club also wanted to get a key to the pavilion we might want to know who were the club's office bearers and what was the financial position of the club (in case there was any problem about damage to the pavilion). And if we were advising the local council on whether the club should get one of the sport development grants that the council was making available to sports clubs, we might want to be sure that the club kept proper accounts, and that it actually did play tennis.

In this way we are recognising that an organisation is not a clear and unambiguous object, something that's either there or not there. Rather it is something that we recognise by applying our understanding to the things that people do. The aim of this book is to sharpen that understanding and to turn it into a systematic and conscious part of the reader's repertoire of skills. Its concern is with organisation in operation: it asks 'what is it, and why does it matter?' It is concerned with different ways of organising, as this is particularly relevant in our thinking about many public policy questions. For instance, should the care of old people be left to their families? Should the government provide care? Or should it be left to private providers to identify and fill this commercial opportunity? These are questions about alternative ways of organising.

This is not the only approach that can be taken to organisation. There are distinctive approaches in several academic disciplines, such as sociology, political science and economics. There are bodies of specialists, writing on organisational questions relating to a particular functional area (e.g. educational administration or health administration). And the enormous literature on management is, in a sense, concerned with the application of our knowledge about organisation.

All of these bodies of writing have their own ways of raising significant questions, and looking for answers. This book has its focus on what people do – on the *process* of organisation. It is not concerned to categorise particular organisations at the start (e.g. into formal and informal organisations), and it keeps an open mind about whether people use organisations to pursue goals, or even whether they need to be acting deliberately to sustain organisation.

So, rather than starting with a definition of a set of categories, we will start with a broad question about the organisational process. What makes us recognise something as 'organisation'? What is it that's happening when people organise? Take, for instance, the way that a university student's course of study is organised: we can recognise three different ways in which this happens.

One way is by the use of *authorised rules*. There will be university or faculty rules governing what students may include in their degree, and these may be used to make sure that students take particular units – for instance, they may require students to include one unit of a foreign language.

Alternatively, it may be left to the students' perception of their own *self-interest* to decide what to study. Those who think their job prospects will be better if they have credit for some foreign language will study it; those who don't think it will help them will not.

Or the choices that students make about which subjects to study will reflect *norms and values* – that is, understandings about what you do at university that are widely shared – among students and among 'relevant others', including academic staff, parents, school teachers and non-university friends. These may include ideas about 'a reasonable spread of subjects' or 'a good general education.' They may mean that students do what their friends would approve of (so that students majoring in economics are likely to take supporting units in computing or accounting, and unlikely to take units in philosophy or biology).

We have identified the following three ways in which a student's course selection can be organised. Each of them rests on a different assumption about how the actions of individuals can best be related to one another:

- people follow authoritative rules
- people make their own calculations about what's in their best interests
- people are sensitive to the expectations of others.

We will go on to see how these assumptions can be developed into models of organisation that are useful in the analysis of actual cases.

Review

1. Organisation is a result of people's shared ideas about how they should act in particular circumstances.
2. Informal organisation may supplement or substitute for formal organisation.
3. Activity may be more or less organised.
4. This book is concerned with the process of organising.
5. Organisation is the result of the application of authorised rules, self-interest or shared norms and values.

Questions for Discussion

1. What similarities and differences do you notice between the organisation of the following?

   - secondary school and university/college
   - employment and secondary school
   - family and university/college.

2. What are the formal and informal elements in the organisation of a school, university/college department? Do these elements reinforce or undermine each other?
3. What alternative ways are there of organising child care?

4. How is 'organisation' dealt with in other subjects or courses you have taken, and in what ways does it differ from the approach in this chapter?
5. Identify examples of 'authorised rules', 'self-interest' and 'shared norms and values' in the following organised activities:

    *   looking for a job
    *   organising a dance party
    *   getting married
    *   joining a political movement.

Further Reading

On rules see Hood (1986: 17–47). On norms see Elster (1989: 113–123). On interests see Hindess (1989: 66–85).

2　Why Organise?

If we are trying to explain organisation it would seem sensible to begin by asking why we have organisation in the first place. This was the approach taken by the political philosopher Thomas Hobbes, who asked 'what would life be like if we didn't have government – if we lived in a "state of nature"?'

In this chapter we take some (largely hypothetical) cases and ask 'do cases like this call for organisation?' and 'do they present problems for organisation?' We can then move on to look at ways of organising as possible responses to these demands for organisation.

Draining the Meadow

Two neighbours may agree to drain a meadow, which they possess in common: because it is easy for them to know each other's mind; and each must perceive that the immediate consequence of his failing in his part is the abandoning the whole project. But it is very difficult, and indeed impossible, that a thousand persons should agree in any such action; it being difficult for them to concert so complicated a design, and still more difficult for them to execute it; while each seeks a pretext to free himself of the trouble and expense, and would lay the whole burden on others. (Hume, 1911: 239)

The philosopher David Hume's example of 'draining the meadow' was first written in 1739 and remains a good illustration of the difficulties of acting collectively with other people. Often we would be better off if we did things together rather than as individuals, but effective organisation doesn't always happen. Hume points to four dimensions of the difficulty of organising.

First, there is the problem of knowing what is required for joint action: what do I have to do? And what are the others going to do? It is relatively easy, Hume says, for two neighbours to know what each has to do in order to accomplish some common purpose, but much harder for everyone in a larger group to have the same mutual understanding.

Second, there is the problem of getting everyone to want to act together. Hume assumes that people are basically selfish: they will seek to avoid 'trouble and expense', if they can get away with it. Given a choice, people will do less rather than more, particularly if they can get someone else to fill the gap, and if they do choose to do something it is because they expect to get something out of it.

This 'common sense' assumption that people are motivated by calculations of how to get the most benefit for the least effort – i.e. that they are rational, self-interested utility-maximisers – underlies modern (so-called 'neoclassical') economic theory, and matches our perception of ourselves as rational, no-nonsense people. If someone is doing something, there must be something in it for them. If they're not doing it for money, it must be for the satisfaction they get out of it, or some other form of benefit. So organised relationships can be understood as the result of a prior agreement (or 'social contract') to act collectively because of the benefits that this will bring to individuals.

The third question is who will benefit from the collective activity. Hume suggests that one of the difficulties with draining the meadow is that it is owned 'in common'. A single owner might be more motivated to do the work, or more willing to pay others to do it, knowing that he or she will reap the benefits in the long run. This is why it is argued that privately owned enterprises are likely to be more productive than those that are collectively owned: people will work harder for themselves than they will for some group of which they are a part, because they can be sure that they will get the benefit of their effort. Arguments about incentives and ownership underlie the debate about privatisation and the role of the state that has spread through most countries, including the former Soviet Union, since the early 1980s.

Finally, there is the number of people involved: 'two neighbours', Hume suggests, are more likely to be successful than 'a thousand persons' in agreeing how to proceed, and in monitoring each other's contribution to the work. They can act collectively without any evident 'organisation', and this might still be the case if there were four or five of them, but if there were four or five hundred, collective action would be difficult without some form of organisation – that is, some agreed way of acting together which was known in advance. It is the problem of coordinating the actions of a large number of people – for example students in a university – with which this book (and indeed all of organisation studies) is concerned.

We can see here the core of the problem of organisation: the divergence between the self-interest of the individual and the demands of collective action, and the inter-relationship between what one individual does and what all the others do. This 'core problem' can be seen in some of the 'classic dilemmas' of organisation, like 'free-riding' and the 'tragedy of the commons'.

Free riding

Organising for collective action takes effort – time, or money, or energy – and we assume that people are prepared to invest this effort because of the benefit that they will get out of it. But what if they can get the benefit without having to invest the effort – that is, to have a 'free ride'?

The economist Mancur Olson looked into this question. He was puzzled by people's reluctance to join organisations, even if membership seemed to be in their interests. Consumer boycotts or trade unions, for example, had difficulty attracting members, even if they were effective in lowering prices or negotiating pay increases. Olson argued that as the number of members of an organisation grows, the effect of each additional contribution becomes smaller, and so the incentive to 'free ride' increases. People will feel that their membership won't make any difference, and that they'll get the benefit, whether they join or not. So they fail to join, or let their membership lapse. From each individual's point of view, it makes sense not to join.

Of course, if everyone followed this logic no one would join, and one question that comes out of Olson's work is why anyone joins one of these associations. One possibility is compulsion, e.g. the 'union shop', where membership in the union is a condition of employment and union subscriptions are deducted from the pay packet.

But Olson assumes that people will remain free to choose, and suggests that it is therefore necessary to offer 'selective incentives' available only to those who join the organisation. The trade union will have to restrict pay increases to its members, or provide cheap holidays or housing loans that are available only to members, if it is going to persuade people to join and stay. Otherwise they will 'free ride'. They will benefit from the pay increases won by the union, but they will not bother joining because (they reason) one member more or less will not make a difference.

The Tragedy of the Commons

This possibility of a divergence between the collective interests of the group and the interests of each individual member becomes particularly important in the management of 'open access resources', such as the air and the sea. Garrett Hardin (1968) imagined a pasture owned in common by a number of people – a village, perhaps – with all members having the right to use it. A number of farmers let their animals graze on the pasture. If too many farmers do this, the number of animals will exceed the capacity of the pasture to feed them, and the pasture will be destroyed by over-use. But from each farmer's point of view, one more animal put out to graze will not make much difference. The farmer will benefit immediately and directly from grazing the animal. The shared costs of land degradation will show up only in the longer term, and be divided up among all the farmers.

Hardin argued that there was a permanent tension between individual and collective interests in the use of open access resources. He called this 'the tragedy of the commons'. The argument also applies to fisheries, where over-fishing may result in the complete disappearance of the fish. Later in the book we will examine this question in relation to another open access resource, the airwaves used in broadcasting radio and TV.

There are two ways of organising which are seen as responses to the tragedy of the commons:

- some external authority is introduced to over-ride individual choice, which we might call *regulation;* or
- ownership of the commons is divided among the users, which we might call *privatisation.*

Regulation would mean setting up some kind of central, hierarchical authority to control access to the commons. It would in some way decide what the carrying capacity of the commons was, and allocate licences among the farmers who wanted to use it. Some kind of policing would have to be introduced to prevent farmers using more than their licensed access, and to exclude the unlicensed. In this way, authority would be used to over-ride self-interest.

Alternatively, it is argued, self-interest can be mobilised to protect the common, by dividing it among the users, with each user responsible for an individual plot. This approach sees the source of the 'tragedy of the commons' as the divergence between incentive and ownership. Because they didn't own the land individually, the farmers would not take individual responsibility for it. The privatisation approach seeks to change the structure of ownership, on the assumption that people will better look after things they own. If the pasture is subdivided into individual farms then each owner may think twice before putting more animals out to graze, as the costs of overgrazing will fall directly on him or her (or their descendants, if the ownership is heritable).

Elinor Ostrom argues that these two organisational responses to the tragedy of the commons – regulation (the appeal to authority) and privatisation (the appeal to self-interest) – do not exhaust the possibilities. She argues that people are capable of recognising the problem, and harnessing the self-interested behaviour of individuals, without recourse to central authority or the market, and cites a numbers of cases of groups working out ways of managing common property without the use of outside authority. These all involve people recognising their collective interest as well as their individual interest, and imposing restrictions on each other in order to safeguard their common property. So we need to add to privatisation and regulation a third possible organisational response, one we might call *collective self-restraint*.

What we are seeing here are examples of three distinct ways of organising: appealing to authority (regulation), appealing to self-interest (privatisation), and in the last case (collective self-restraint) appealing to people's sense of belonging to a group – that is, to affiliation.

We can see these ways of organising in a range of contexts. To take a micro-level example, we might think of a group of students who have moved into a house together and are addressing the question of how the common areas of the house – the kitchen and the bathroom especially – are to be kept clean. They might feel that their sense of mutual obligation to one another will ensure that everyone does some cleaning-up when it's needed – that is, they might rely on affiliation to the group. But they might feel that they could not rely on everyone doing their share, and make a rule that everyone had to take a turn – that is, rely on people's deference to authoritative rules. Or they might try to put a price on having a clean house, perhaps by offering a lower rent to those who were willing to clean the house, or perhaps by charging everyone a higher rent and paying someone to do the cleaning. Either way, they are approaching a collective task via self-interested individual exchange.

The Prisoner's Dilemma

There seem to be some situations where behaviour that is rational for any individual can be disastrous for all those individuals as a group. This has been set out in a formal model known as the 'prisoner's dilemma', based on the following story:

> Two suspects are taken into custody and separated. The District Attorney is certain that they are guilty of a specific crime, but he does not have the evidence to convict them at a trial. He points out to each prisoner that each has two alternatives: to confess to the crime the police are sure they have done, or not to confess. If they both do not confess, then the district attorney states he will book them on some very minor trumped up charge such as petty larceny and illegal possession of a weapon, and they will both receive minor punishment; if they both confess they will both be prosecuted, but he will recommend a less than the most severe sentence; but if one confesses and the other does not, then the confessor will receive lenient treatment for turning state's evidence whereas the latter will get 'the book' slapped at him. (Luce and Raiffa, 1957: 217)

The District Attorney has set up the prisoners to confess. Unable to communicate, they cannot reassure each other that they will not confess. Fearing the worst, the most prudent course for each of them is to confess before the other does.

For the student of organisation, the prisoner's dilemma points to the importance for collective action of knowing what other people will do. In other words, it is not simply that people face a choice between their individual interests and the interests of the organisation: it is that organisation may offer a way of safeguarding individual interests against the uncertain behaviour of others. Seeing the alternatives, individuals might prefer to surrender their power of choice to the state, which will prevent either side from defecting. (Town planning controls offer a good example.) This enables collective action at a fairly basic level. Most forms of organisation call for more than this: the participants need to have developed sufficient trust to be confident that if they cooperate, the others will not seize the short-term advantage to be gained from defecting. So trust becomes an important element of organisation.

River Pollution as an Organisational Problem

Thinking about organisation in this formal, rather abstract way helps us to understand the nature of the problem. Let us take as an example the pollution of a major river (a major policy problem in a number of countries). The river is a common to which everyone has access: factories and farms and stormwater drains all contribute to the pollution. Everyone has an interest in a cleaner river, but for all of the users – factory owners, farmers, local councils – reduction of their contribution to the pollution would impose a cost on them. If every farmer (for instance) bears this cost, they are all equally affected (and may be able to raise their prices to cover it). But if some farmers reduce their pollution (and increase their costs) and others do not, then the ones that do will be at a competitive disadvantage.

Moreover, pollution is not always easy to trace. In the farmer's case, it may simply be the consequence of intense use of agricultural chemicals. We may know that the phosphate level in the river is rising, but where is it coming from? How would we know what any individual farmer was doing? Could we believe what the farmer told us? From the farmer's point of view, he/she may be able to clean up his/her act, at a price, but if all other farmers are doing it too, that price would be acceptable. If they all clean up their act, and he/she doesn't, probably no one could tell the difference.

But if there is still no appreciable reduction in the pollution level, the government may impose a total ban on the use of the chemicals that cause the problem. We can see here the elements of the prisoner's dilemma, and the interplay of trust, coercion and relative advantage in sustaining organisational arrangements.

So, dealing with the problem of river pollution means finding a way of organising land use, and we can imagine several different approaches, just as our students had several alternatives for cleaning their house. Tough new laws could be enacted to limit discharges into the river – i.e organising through authoritative rules. There could be a massive public relations and consciousness-raising campaign to make people aware of the consequences of discharging waste into the river in an attempt to change behaviour – i.e appealing to people's sense of affiliation. Or the government could calculate how much pollution the river could bear, and auction 'licences to pollute' to those willing to pay for them. There would be those who had calculated that it would be cheaper to pay for a licence than to clean up their act; this would establish a market price for pollution, and organise the land use through calculations of self-interest.

But while we can identify these as 'alternatives', it does not follow that they are 'options' that people can pick up as they please. There are already patterns of land use, and ways of dealing with water quality. These may or may not be sufficient to deal with the present task, but they have gained acceptance over time and cannot be ignored. And people's acceptance of new organisational arrangements is shaped by their previous experience. A successful mobilisation of community sentiment to clean up the harbour may encourage people to appeal to affiliation in dealing with river pollution. Conversely, if a set of government-imposed rules to control the spraying of agricultural chemicals turned out to be totally unworkable, people would be reluctant to accept new rules relating to discharge of wastes.

Organisation as Problem Solving

In our discussion so far we have treated organisation as something that people create in response to a need – that is, we have assumed instrumental rationality. This has been convenient for pursuing the argument, but we now need to unpack the assumptions. The argument has assumed that:

- in the beginning, there was no organisation
- there was a problem which was independent of organisation
- rational individuals sought an outcome which gave them the greatest benefit for the least cost
- to do this, they contracted with one another to create the organisation
- organisation can therefore be understood as a way of delivering predetermined benefits to the people involved.

There is nothing particularly wrong with these assumptions as long as we remember that they are assumptions, and that they rest more on the fact that they fit the dominant view of the world and our place in it than on factual evidence. These assumptions are challenged by factually based argument that:

- organisation is a continuing activity; even if we can identify a 'beginning', most people in the organisation weren't around at the time, and even those who were may not have a clear idea of what motivated them at the time, and aren't necessarily driven by that now
- although we can speak of organisation as a means of achieving some collective purpose, it is often remarkably difficult to define what that purpose is: organisational participants may have difficulty

defining objectives, and when they do, they may articulate multiple, overlapping and possibly conflicting purposes
- this fuzziness about purpose is less serious than it might appear because there are clearly other cues for action in organisations, such as professional training, and the expectations of significant others like co-workers or clients: people may not need to know the purposes in order to be regarded as effective members of the organisation
- people may show little interest in determining whether an organisation has achieved its purposes, or abolishing an organisation which appears to have done so, and it seems clear that people value organisations for more than the delivery of pre-determined benefits.

In fact, there are many restraints, both internal and external, on an individual's ability to choose rationally. The choices open to any individual are not always clear, nor are their consequences necessarily known, but people may still have to choose. In any case, people have a limited ability to absorb and compute information. They might not want all the information necessary to make an informed choice. They want to shop cheaply rather than expensively, but they do not check the prices of all the items they want at all the available sources before they buy. Herbert Simon (1976), who explored this phenomenon, called it 'bounded rationality'. Individuals, he said, are rarely presented with full and unambiguous information, and – after a certain point – they stop trying to look for it. Generally, Simon argues, they 'satisfice' rather than 'maximise'. They look for a minimum satisfactory solution rather than the best possible. And their search is guided and constrained by mental maps that derive from their culture, upbringing and experience: 'we usually shop here' or ' the supermarket is usually cheaper'. They do not want to think about all the possibilities every time they do something, as long as what they are doing seems within sensible bounds. So some choices will not be considered, and some things may be done without there having been much of a choice.

Feldman and March (1981) argue that people in organisations regard it as more important to have given the appearance of acting rationally than actually to go through all the steps required to do so. They will ask for more information about alternatives, for example, but not take that information into account. Showing that you are committed to a rational process is more important than going through with it. Rationality is a way of legitimating action, rather than prescribing it.

With these cautions in mind, we can now turn to consider 'what happens when organisation happens', and to do this we will set out our three models of organisation.

Review

1. One approach to understanding organisation is imagining what life would be like without it.
2. Hume's image of 'draining a meadow' identifies four problems that occur when more than two people try to act together:

   - agreeing what must be done
   - overcoming tendencies to laziness and shirking
   - identifying beneficiaries
   - coordinating and monitoring work.

3. A core problem for organisation is divergence between individual self-interest and the requirements of collective action.
4. There is a temptation to 'free ride' when people benefit from organisation, whether or not they participate.
5. If each individual calculates that his or her absence will not make a difference to the outcome, then no-one may join, and everyone loses.
6. The tragedy of the commons occurs in 'open access resources' when users calculate that their own over-exploitation of the resource will benefit them privately, but the costs of over-exploitation will be shared with their neighbours.
7. The tragedy of the commons can be averted by centralised regulation, privatisation of ownership, or decentralised systems of collective self-restraint.
8. In the prisoner's dilemma two prisoners are induced to confess, even though they would both have got away with a lighter sentence if they had both stayed silent. The dilemma represents a class of circumstances in which the outcome depends on the action of others.
9. Cleaning up a river is in some ways like a prisoner's dilemma: there are strong incentives to defect from an agreement that would leave everyone better off.
10. Choices among arrangements are shaped by historical experience as well as by calculations about the future.

11. We do not have to assume that organisations are best understood as the result of agreements between individuals to provide themselves with benefits they could achieve separately (though this is a common assumption).

Questions for Discussion

1. In what circumstances is it sensible to assume that people are rational, self-interested maximisers? What alternative assumptions might we use, with what consequences?
2. What evidence can you find for, and against, the assumption that privately owned enterprises are more productive than publicly owned enterprises?
3. In relation to which organisations are you a 'free rider', and how could you be induced to join?
4. What 'tragedies of the commons' can you identify around the school or university/college campus?
5. What is your preferred solution to the tragedy of the commons, and why do you favour it?
6. How could the prisoners beat the district attorney?
7. In what ways does the history of previous organisational arrangements constrain the choice of alternatives in education?
8. Are you a member of any organisations that were created as the results of contracts between individuals to provide themself with benefits they could not achieve separately?
9. What are the purposes of the organisation in which you are studying, and how do you know what they are?

Further Reading

Hood (1986) and Laver (1983) explain organisation from individualistic first principles. Ostrom (E) (1990) develops the idea and gives empirical examples of self-managed 'common pool resources' (and is critical of the use of models by policy makers). Nicholson (1970: 51–66), Schotter (1985: 47–64) Zagare (1984), Pettitt (1985), Weale (1990: 205–209) and McLean (1986: 126–148) explain the basic ideas of game theory, including the prisoner's dilemma. Blinder (1987: 136–159) discusses 'market' solutions to environmental pollution. Weick (1979) and March and Feldman (1988) criticise the idea of organisations as problem solving.

3   Models of Organisation

We saw at the end of Chapter 1 that people may act together for a variety of reasons: because they think that it's in their interest; because they're following the rules; or because that's what everyone does. In Chapter 2 we found three responses to the tragedy of the commons: private ownership; regulation by an external authority; and self-restraint by appeal to people's sense of belonging to a group.

In this chapter we explore more elaborate models of organisation that correspond to each of these three reasons or responses, as shown in Table 3.1. Then we use them to analyse more realistic cases of organisation in Chapters 5–7.

Table 3.1

Reason for action (see Chapter 1)	Response to the 'tragedy of the commons' (see Chapter 2)	Model of organisation	Organising principles
'In my interest'	Private ownership	Market	Incentives, prices
'Following rules'	External authority	Bureaucracy	Rules, authority hierarchy
'Everyone does' it this way	Collective self restraint	Community	Norms, values, affiliation, networks

The models, here called 'market', 'bureaucracy' and 'community', are widely used in the social sciences, sometimes with different labels. Economists have been particularly preoccupied with markets, and political scientists with bureaucracy, while sociologists have theorised about all three. The models are not the exclusive property of any particular discipline. They are also part of the everyday mental baggage of politicians and government officials.

We have identified three models. Other analysts use fewer, or more. Our preference for 'market', 'bureaucracy' and 'community' comes from a dissatisfaction with the simple alternatives of 'state' and 'market' that were proposed during the 1980s, and a feeling that additional models,

such as 'family', 'networks' and 'associations' were really just variations
of what we call 'commmunity'. Rather than invent our own jargon,
we use the words 'market', 'bureaucracy' and 'community' to describe
models of organisation based on self-interest, rules and affiliation.
Students need to be alert to the fact that other analysts, and different
disciplines, may define them differently, and make different distinc-
tions.

Before looking at them in detail we need to note some of their characteristics as models. The first point is that *models are constructs*. They
are abstract and simplified representations of reality which highlight some
aspects rather than others.

Second, *models are tools*, constructed for particular purposes. These
purposes may be descriptive of what is or prescriptive of what should
be. Here we are using models of organisation for the purposes of
analysis and comparison.

Third, in analysing organisation, *more than one model may be useful*. In
particular cases, there may be more than one way in which people
organise, and more than one model may be needed to analyse the organisational process adequately.

Fourth, the models are *not completely distinct*: some elements of one
also appear in another.

Fifth, there is a *trade off between simplicity and realism*. Models must
simplify, and may over-simplify. Each organisation is in some ways
unique, but all share some common features.

Fifth, a particular feature of organisational models is that *the people
whose activities are being modelled are also users of models*. Sometimes people
act out of unconscious routine, but at other times they use their own
models to orient themselves, to plan what to do next, and to justify their
actions to themselves and to persuade others to follow them. Players
usually know the rules of the game (even if they sometimes ignore, mis-
interpret, forget or disagree about them). Government officials have their
own ideas of bureaucracy, business managers have their own ideas
about 'the market', and local politicians have their own ideas about how
'communities' work. They use models to mobilise others behind them.
Faced with a problem, some people call for 'more rules' (in our terms
'bureaucracy'), others for 'more incentives' (in our terms 'market'), while
others call for more regard for other each others' feelings (in our terms
'community').

Students of organisation therefore need to know what models are being
used by the participants, as this will (at least in part) help explain the
outcome. The participant's account of the organisational process is

likely to be significantly different from that of the student. Participants have a partial and partisan view of the action: that is, they see only a part of the action, and they make sense of it in terms of their own interests.

Market

We will use the word 'market' to describe a model of the world driven entirely by calculations of self-interest. The term is mostly used in relation to commercial transactions, but it can be applied to social life generally. Should motorcyclists be required to wear helmets, for example, or should it be left to their own judgement of their best interests?

The market model holds not only that individuals are the best judges of their own best interests, but that the best result for society as a whole comes from everyone pursuing their own interests. Writing in the eighteenth century, the political economist Adam Smith argued that the outcome of such self-interested choices – e.g. by people wanting to buy things and people wanting to sell things – is that there is a flow of goods for sale at prices that people are prepared to pay. In this way, argued Smith, the self-interested individual is led:

> as if by an invisible hand to provide an end which was not part of his intention. Nor is it always the worse for the society that it was not part of it. By pursuing his own interests, he frequently promotes that of the society more effectually than when he really intends to promote it. (Cited in Alt and Chrystal, 1983: 15)

Most people have some experience of the sort of markets that sell fruit and vegetables. We know that they are ways of bringing together buyers and sellers, that no one is obviously in charge, and that what is available will depend on mutual understanding reached between buyers and sellers. Sellers may buy bananas from the growers in the expectation that buyers will want them at the price asked. If they find that shoppers are reluctant to buy, they may cut the price, particularly just before the close of trading on Saturday. On the other hand, if for any reason not many bananas get thought to the market this week, the price is likely to rise.

Modern economics has elaborated a particular model of the market. In a 'freely competitive' market, say the economists,

- there is a large number of buyers and sellers
- they know what they want

- they are able to pay for it
- they act independently of each other
- they are free to enter and leave the market
- information about products and prices is free and accessible
- there are no costs in making deals.

Adam Smith was primarily concerned with commercial trading, but the market model has a much wider application. Should there be an art gallery in this city? Yes, proponents of the market model might say, if people want it, and are willing to pay an admission charge which would cover the costs of building it and running it. If not enough people want to visit the gallery, or if those who do cannot pay the price, then there will be no gallery – nor should there be.

Bureaucracy

While we may rely on the workings of individual self-interest to ensure the supply of hot dogs at a football match, we do not assume that this will operate to keep down speeding on the roads. For this, we rely on laws in which people do things because someone further up the line has directed them to do so. In this case, parliament passes a law defining speed limits, and the police commissioner directs police to apprehend and prosecute offenders. The police officer who books a speeding motorist is not pursuing his/her own self-interest, but recognising the hierarchical authority of the parliament and the police commissioner.

If the organisation in which all transactions were governed by self-interest could be called a market, the organisation in which all transactions were governed by the hierarchical application of rules might be called a bureaucracy. Our understanding of bureaucracy owes much to the pioneering work of the sociologist Max Weber who drew attention to the way in which more personal styles of administration, centred on the king, queen or chief and those he or she trusted, were supplanted by 'rational/legal' organisational structures, which were staffed by full-time officials appointed to their careers on the basis of their qualifications, and whose jobs were circumscribed by rules.

The political scientist Christopher Hood (1976) has developed a model of 'perfect administration' (comparable to the economists' model of a 'freely competitive market'), outlining the features of an organisation entirely governed by the hierarchical application of rules:

- the organisation is unitary, not subdivided into parts
- its members share the same norms and values
- the members are perfectly obedient
- there is full information about the problems the organisation has to deal with
- members have all the time they need to do their job properly.

Community

The third possible basis for people to act together is affiliation: people can act in concert because they are doing what is appropriate for members of some larger grouping. This grouping may be a national society. Queuing, for instance, is one way in which people can act together because 'everyone knows' what appropriate behaviour is. What is seen to be appropriate varies from one national society to another: queuing in one country might be quite different from queuing in another. So when people go to other countries, they know that practices like queuing may work quite differently from the way they are used to, and watch to see what the 'local rules' are. The grouping may be an ethnic group within a national society, or a recognised profession: doctors, for instance, deal individually with patients, but they are guided and constrained by what other doctors would do. Here, the source of the collective action is not their self-interest or a rule, but their affiliation to a wider collectivity called 'doctors'.

The organisation where relations are governed by a common affiliation is community. The term implies a group of people who have something in common which makes them want to act in the same way: 'shared norms and values' is a popular way of putting it.

The model of 'community' was used by Ferdinand Tönnies (1957) to draw attention to the changes that were happening to European societies as a consequence of industrialisation. He argued that in pre-industrial society, village life was characterised by physical proximity and frequent interaction with other people who were known to you, and this facilitated the development and persistence of shared norms and values. He referred to this sort of society as *Gemeinschaft* ('community') and contrasted it with the relatively anonymous, impersonal, contractual world of industrial society, which he called *Gesellschaft* ('association').

The 'loss of community' theme has attracted many other writers since Tönnies; it seems to tap a shared sentiment. This discussion often overlooks the way in which such groupings as the 'counter-culture', the 'moral majority', the 'women's movement' or the 'gay community' also draw on the sense of affiliation which Tönnies saw in the pre-industrial village. And as we have seen, one of the bases for organisation among professionals like doctors is their sense of affiliation to the profession as a whole.

The concept of community has also been used to make sense of the maintenance of complex relationships involving people from different organisations. Heclo and Wildavsky (1974), for instance, argued that 'Treasury control' in British government could only be understood in terms of the relationships of trust which grew up among the 'expenditure community', and there is a large body of writing on the idea of the 'policy community'. Some writers prefer the term 'network', defined by Thompson et al (1991: 14) as 'informal relationships between essentially equal social agents and agencies', but in terms of our analysis they are talking about the same thing: relationships based on affiliation rather than hierarchy or self-interested exchange.

The political theorist Michael Taylor has developed a model of 'community' which we can put alongside our models of the perfect market and the perfect bureaucracy. Taylor's model identifies three essential elements of a community. The first is common values and beliefs. The second is that relationships between members should be direct and many sided, rather than indirect and specialised. The third is that transactions within the community are characterised by reciprocity: the expectation that if I help you now, you will help me in future (1982: 26–30).

Taylor (1982: 91) draws many of his examples from anthropological accounts of Melanesian societies, where community is maintained by:

- the threat of 'self-help' retaliation
- the offer of reciprocity and the threat of its withdrawal
- the use of sanctions of approval and disapproval, the latter especially via gossip, ridicule and shaming
- the threat of witchcraft accusations and of supernatural sanctions.

Taylor's model is also relevant to modern industrial societies. While the police and courts have supplanted some forms of 'self-help' retaliation, we still recognise some circumstances in which it is right to 'take the law into our own hands'. We often practise reciprocity by helping neighbours or workmates in the expectation that we may call on them for help in future. We gossip as a way of discouraging inappropriate behaviour. And we sometimes invoke supernatural rewards and sanctions (Santa Claus or God) to socialise children into the community of adults.

Table 3.2 summarises the characteristics of the three models.

Table 3.2

Bureaucracy (from Hood, 1976)

- Unitary organisation
- Uniformity of norms and values
- Perfect obedience
- Full information
- Time to consider

Market

- Many buyers and sellers
- They know what they want
- They can pay for it
- They act independently
- They are free to enter and exit
- Information is freely available
- No costs in making and keeping agreements

Community
(From Taylor, 1982)

- Common beliefs and values
- Direct, many-sided relationships
- Reciprocity
- Threats of self-help retaliation
- Use of gossip, shaming and supernatural sanctions

Using Models in Analysis

We need to be able to dissect areas of organisation and see how it has been put together – and here our three models are useful. Take, for example, the way that caring for young children is organised. The parents of young children often want to have them cared for by someone else, perhaps to enable the parents to go out to work (in which case it is usually called 'child care'), perhaps to enable them to go out in the evening (when the caring is called 'babysitting'). This is accomplished through a complex and varied pattern of arrangements, ranging from a formal child care centre to 'leaving the kids with Grandma for a couple of hours'.

In other words, caring for children is organised in a variety of ways, and the models can help us to be more precise in our analysis of this organisational field. We can identify a 'market' pattern, where caring for children is a service which is bought by people who need it, and the nature of the service is determined by what the seller is offering and what the buyer needs or can afford. Alternatively, there could be a 'bureaucratic' form of provision, in which child care of a prescribed type is provided by an organisation (probably governmental, but conceivably an employer or trade union) in accordance with a set of rules governing entitlements. Or there could be a 'community' form, in which the caring is done on the basis of shared membership in a relevant group, e.g. by a relative or neighbour.

Having used the models of organisation to identify the different possibilities, we can then look at actual cases, and use the models to clarify the organisational characteristics of the activity of child care, and to make comparisons. We can see that making an arrangement with a neighbour draws more on the community model, whereas the centre run by the local council is more bureaucratic in nature.

We can make comparisons between different times and localities. We might note, for instance, that with the changing nature of the family and the increasing participation of women in the paid workforce, there is less reliance on community (particularly family) and more on bureaucratic provision (usually by government, but also by employers). We might also note that there is more bureaucratic provision during the day, and more reliance on market provision in the evenings. In analysing this, we might note that it is easier to hire carers at night (since many teenagers who are at school in the day are willing to mind children in the evenings), and also that it is easier to get political support for child care which enables mothers to go to work than for care which enables mothers to go to the pictures.

We might also note the way that patterns of child care change their character: 'leaving the child with a neighbour' is formally recognised by the government and becomes Family Day Care, with standards and fees regulated by the local council. Informal arrangements among parents become babysitting cooperatives with defined rules and entitlements.

In other words, when we recognise that caring for children is accomplished through a complex organisational pattern, using our models can help us to describe and analyse these patterns.

We can also see that people draw on these models to change organised arrangements. For instance, soft drink cans are convenient to the user, but if they are discarded in the street they may be a nuisance to other people, who may seek to take collective action to do something about it – in other words, to re-cast the organisational arrangements relating to soft drinks. One way of doing this might be to introduce more stringent rules about littering. Another might be setting up a scheme to buy used cans. A third might be an advertising campaign calling on people to 'Do the Right Thing' and put their empty cans in a rubbish bin. The first scheme is more bureaucratic in character and relies on people obeying rules. The second is more market oriented, and assumes that if there's money in it, someone will pick up the cans. The third is community oriented, and relies on an appeal to shared norms. People may appeal to any of these principles, and the outcome is likely to be an alloy, as it were, though the reform may be a change in the nature of the alloy or mixture: more reliance on self-interest, for instance, and less on rules.

We can see, then, that the models are quite 'practical', though the people using them to bring about changes may not be conscious of the way they are using abstract models. They may refer to them in a common-sense way (e.g. 'this is all becoming too bureaucratic') but might be quite surprised to be told that they are drawing on abstract models of organisation.

Review

1. Models are abstract constructions: more than one may be useful for analysing any particular case.
2. The economists' 'freely competitive market' provides a model of the world driven entirely by self-interest.
3. Hood's 'perfect administration' provides a model of bureaucracy driven by the hierarchical application of rules.
4. Taylor provides a model of community driven by self-help, reciprocity and gossip.
5. Activities like child care can be organised by markets, bureaucracy or community: in practice there is a mixture of these forms.

6. The three models can also be used to make comparison between different activities, times and places.
7. Social actors themselves use models to propose solutions to problems.

Questions for Discussion

1. What are the elements of the model of 'student' and 'teacher' that underlie the organisation of education?
2. In what ways do actual students and teachers differ from these models?
3. Use the models of 'student' and 'teacher' to discuss the differences and similarities between:

   * secondary school and university/college
   * lectures and other forms of teaching
   * different subjects or disciplines in the school or university/college
   * education in other countries
   * education now and in the past.

4. To what extent is education organised according to the following?

   * the economists' 'freely competitive market'
   * Hood's 'perfect administration'
   * Taylor's 'community'.

5. Use the three models to analyse the provision of care for elderly people.
6. Identify examples from the newspaper of people advocating 'market' 'bureaucratic' and 'community' solutions to public problems.

Further Reading

Rigby (1964,1990) uses 'command', 'custom' and 'contract', described as 'modes of coordinating social activity', in his analysis of former Soviet society. Streeck and Schmitter (1985: 1–29) analyse the properties of three 'models of social order' (community, market and state) before introducing a fourth 'associative' model which they link to 'corporatism'. Butler (1983) considers them as forms of control. Hamilton and Biggart (1988) apply the three models to newly industrialising countries in East Asia, and Larmour (1990) applies them to land tenure in Melanesia.

The market model is explained further in Friedman and Friedman (1980: 9–37), and Heilbroner and Thurow (1982: 157–178).

The community model is explained as a form of anarchy in Laver (1983: 147–66), and as a network by Marchment and Thompson, eds (1993).

The bureaucratic model is explained by Weber (1991), and defended by Goodsell (1986) and Jacques (1991).

4   Failures of the Models

Simply to set out these models is to realise the extent of the gap between them and practice. Hood demonstrated the 'limits of administration' by specifying the conditions of 'unlimited' administration. Economics has some well-developed ideas about the way the world fails to live up to the conditions of its model of freely competitive markets. It calls these failures to meet the conditions of the model 'market failures'. References to 'community' often imply criticisms of the failure of the modern world to live up to earlier standards of kindness and proper behaviour.

In what sense do models 'fail'? As we have seen, they are bound to simplify, and abstract, so must fail the test of 'realism'. Yet we cannot understand reality directly without some models of what to look for. Ordinary language shapes what we recognise and treat as significant (like the Eskimos, who are said to have 20 different words for 'snow'). The specialised jargon of the social and natural sciences tries to make these linguistic models more precise, and more generally applicable.

The question is part of a more general one: is the world orderly, or do we bring order to it? In one sense our models are constructions, which we use to make sense of a reality and explain it to each other. Yet there also seem to be real 'markets', 'bureaucracies' and 'communities' that exist 'out there' whether or not we have models of them.

Part of the answer is that social order is sustained by shared assumptions about how we should act. If everyone shares a model then it is real to the extent that no single person can change it independently. For example, 'real' markets exist because people participating in them agree that it is right and proper that people should act self-interestedly in producing and exchanging goods. They are sustained by the scorn we pour on people who don't play the game (for example by giving things away). And they fail to come into being, for example in parts of the former Soviet Union or in some developing countries, if people do not widely share assumptions about the propriety of self-interested behaviour.

Failure also implies a standard of 'success'. We might not like what bureaucracies do, but we might like them even less if they started acting according to Hood's model. There are other ways of evaluating organisations than by comparing them with our three models, and these will be considered in Chapter 10.

In this chapter we use the phrase 'failure' to refer to the gaps between the expectations of a particular model and the practice of organisation. Borrowing the idea of market failure from economics we shall extend it to include the 'failures' of administration identified by Hood, and the conditions under which community forms of organisation, as defined by Taylor, might 'fail'. We will find that the 'failures' of one model often provide opportunities for the other – for example when hierarchical rules are invoked to correct market failure.

Market Failure

The market model sees the coordination of social activity as being accomplished by private dealing between the individuals involved, but it encounters difficulties when:

- there is only one buyer or seller (monopoly)
- other people are affected, apart from those dealing (externalities)
- people don't know enough to make a deal (information failure)
- the goods in question are not suitable for individual dealing (public goods).

These are then seen as the sources of 'market failure'.

Monopoly

The market model assumes that those who want something, and those who have something to offer, can get together easily: there are no 'barriers to entry' to the market place. If you invent a new mousetrap, you can offer it for sale. If you have a new theory about the origin of the universe, you can try to persuade people of its merits. In each case, the test of success is the response of the consumers: 'the market decides'.

But while it may be relatively easy to set up a factory to make a mousetrap, the more complex and expensive the technology, the more difficult it becomes for new entrants to the market.

'Natural monopolies' emerge where high capital costs form barriers to entry to new competitors, and the existence of networks allows established operators to fight off upstart competitors before they can become established. Examples of natural monopolies typically include electricity supply, telephones, and other utilities supplied through a network. Once an electricity company has established a network it is unusual for a competitor to emerge. Huge investment would be needed to establish a second network, and meanwhile the established operator can afford to compete aggressively on price to prevent new customers signing up with the competitor (and raise prices again once they have been driven off).

The potential for abuse of a natural monopoly is often cited as a reason for government regulation or ownership. The prices charged by public utilities are typically regulated, or the government regulates through owning the utility itself. Recently, however, governments have sought to introduce new investment into public utilities like telecommunications by selling them to private investors. They have relied on newly created regulatory bodies to prevent private absuses of monopolies, or they have encouraged competition by breaking up networks, or encouraging new entrants.

Supporters of 'contestability' such as Harold Demsetz (1968) and William Baumol (1982) argue that the existence of 'natural monopolies' has been overstated, and that the presence of a monopoly is not, of itself, a reason for concern and government action. The issue is whether or not the market is open to contest by new entrants. The possibility of 'hit and run' competition, they argue, will keep the monopolist honest.

Often the monopoly may have its origins in government regulation. The right to treat the sick, for instance, is generally controlled by government regulations. Only those who have followed a particular course of study can be regarded as doctors, and there are restrictions on the ability of others to enter the field, so the ability of sick people to choose between (say) conventional medicine and acupuncture is significantly reduced.

The barriers to entry in the employment field may be more subtle. It may be that for a particular position only those already in the organisation will be considered. Or the job may be structured in such a way that it is difficult for people with responsibility for young children to do it, which has the effect of excluding a large number of women (and a very small number of men) from the job.

Externalities

The second difficulty with relying on agreement between the parties to organise social activity is that not all the people affected are necessarily present. When the soap factory makes a soap powder that people are happy to buy at the advertised price, but the manufacturing process results in a lot of soot and grease being deposited on the clotheslines of the houses surrounding the factory, then the people who live in these houses are carrying part of the cost of production – the damage it does to them. This is referred to by economists as an externality or 'neighbourhood effect'.

The economist Ronald Coase (1960) has argued that the problem of externalities can be dealt with within the market framework through the mobilisation of property rights. If the people who live near the factory have a clear legal right to a quiet neighbourhood or clean air they can sue the polluter if that right is disturbed. Coase's innovation was to see that right as a property right – something that could be bought and sold. Thus the property owners might face a choice: to oppose the factory, or to accept the polluted water or dirty air in exchange for satisfactory compensation. Similarly, a company polluting a river might face a choice to install equipment to clean up its emissions or to buy out the property owners downstream.

But intricate negotiations like this would not be without their own costs. Each of the factory's neighbours would have to calculate how much pollution was acceptable and what compensation would be appropriate, and negotiate an agreement on these lines with the factory owners. Lawyers would have to be hired, expert advice might be needed, documents would have to be checked and, above all, the outcome would have to be monitored to ensure that the agreement was being kept. These are called 'transaction costs', and in this case they could obviously be quite substantial.

The neighbours could reduce their individual transaction costs by banding together, e.g. having one lawyer represent all the neighbours in their dealings with the company. But this would require the neighbours to meet and work out a common position. If they found that they did not agree on how much pollution to accept and how much compensation to demand, they would have to work out a compromise, i.e. some of them would have to sacrifice some of their amenity in the interests of reaching a quick settlement; this, too, is a 'transaction cost'.

The transaction costs in this case might be quite large, and the individual benefits relatively small. In these circumstances, it is argued, market exchange will not be an adequate way of managing the pollution problem, and the state will have to 'intervene' and enforce control through regulation.

Information Failure

The market model assumes that people know what they want, and can make their own decisions about whether or not what they are offered is what they want. But it is argued that in many cases people do not have the technical knowledge to make that judgement. We want to fly on planes that are safe, with pilots who are competent, but most of us do not have any way of judging whether this is so. So we look for an authoritative body, independent of the airline, which can assure us on that point. We can then make an informed choice in terms of the other variables, such as the convenience of the timetable, the comfort of the plane, etc. Government regulations that require manufacturers to put health warnings on cigarettes, or label food with a 'use by' date can also be justified as correcting information failure.

Public Goods

The market model assumes that those who stand to benefit from the provision of a good or service will seek it out and pay for it. If they think it is worth the price asked, they will pay, and it will be supplied. If not, it will not be.

However, there are some goods whose benefits apply to everyone, whether they have asked for them or not, and for which it is difficult to charge people, since they will enjoy the benefit whether they pay for it or not. These are called 'public goods', and the classic examples are defence and street lighting. In these cases the market is said to 'fail', since one could not expect people to pay charges if they got the service whether they paid or not. These services tend to be provided by the state and paid for by compulsory taxation. The name 'public good' is confusing: it does not apply to all the goods supplied by the government, or indeed all the goods that benefit the public (many of which, like food and shelter are provided privately). Public goods have two characteristics:

- one person's enjoyment of them does not detract from another's (non-rivalry)
- no one can be prevented from enjoying them, once they are provided (non-excludability).

The non-rivalry and non-excludability of public goods gives rise to the problem of charging and paying for them. Private goods can be divided up and withheld from people who will not or cannot pay for them. But public goods create opportunities for free riders, who benefit from the good but refuse to pay for it. Because private firms cannot be certain of getting paid, they will be unwilling to invest in providing the public good, or go bankrupt doing so. Hence, it is often argued, the existence of public goods justifies the existence of the state, which can force users to pay for public goods through taxation.

The lighthouse used to be regarded as the typical public good: one ship's benefit from it does not prevent another's (unless it interrupts the line of sight), and ships passing in the night can get away without paying. However, Ronald Coase (1974) argues that, historically, lighthouses have been privately provided, collecting their dues when ships come into dock, (although these charges need to be enforced through state authority) and it is easy to imagine a system of coded signals, like those used for satellite TV pictures, that would allow non-subscribers to be excluded. So the 'publicness' of public goods, and hence the rationale for government ownership, depends much on the costs and technology of charging users. The list of pure public goods may be very small.

Bureaucratic Failure

The bureaucratic model is built on the assumption that decisions will be made at the top and that orders will flow smoothly down the line, but there are many circumstances when this assumption will be misleading.

What subordinates do may not be exactly what their superiors want; this is sometimes called the 'principal-agent' problem. People lower down the line will not necessarily comply with directives from above. They may engage in passive resistance to instructions they do not like, and enforcement of unpopular rules may provoke active resistance. It may be that the instructions from above are far from clear and depend on a great deal of interpretation by those implementing them. Having given the instruction, the principals may have little interest in the subject. In any case, there are practical limits to the amount of control that head office can exercise over its field officers.

Indeed, field staff often have to have a certain amount of autonomy just to do their job: police officers, for instance, and social workers (whom

Michael Lipsky (1978) called 'street level bureaucrats'). Here, professionals represent a problem in a bureaucracy: they are hired because of their specialised knowledge, but with that knowledge comes a claim to autonomy in the way in which it is exercised. A doctor cannot be directed to diagnose in a particular way. And even with non-professionals the existence of specialised knowledge, and the reliance of the centre on that knowledge, limits its capacity to control subordinates. So compliance with central directives is a goal rather than an accomplished fact.

One reason that it is difficult to pass instructions down the line is that there is not a single line but a mass of roughly parallel lines: organisations are divided in specialised segments, each with its own distinctive perspective. Governments are made up of specialised agencies concerned with finance, or education, or forests, or roads. Companies may be divided into production, marketing, sales, finance, industrial relations, etc. In each case, the specialised segments will interpret the messages from the centre in the light of their own specialised knowledge and concerns. They are likely to resist the perspective of the other segments, and to compete with them for resources. In this respect, of course, organisations fail Hood's first test.

Finally, securing collective action through the application of rules requires time and information. Officials want to determine the circumstances of the case, and select the appropriate rule. But information may be incomplete. More often, there is plenty of information but its significance is not obvious, partly because of the specialised and fragmented way in which it is held or becomes available. And officials are typically under pressure to act quickly, without the luxury of reflection or the benefit of long-term planning. In these circumstances, argued Herbert Simon (1976), decision makers in organisations aim for a satisfactory outcome, rather than the best possible one: they are, he argued, not 'maximisers' but 'satisficers'.

Community Failure

One of the difficulties involved in relying on community solidarity as a basis for organisation is the uncertainty about just what 'the community' is, who speaks for it, and to what extent they can commit the other members of the community to particular courses of action. It is easy to invoke the values and preferences of 'the community', but in practice people may feel themselves to be members of a number of overlapping categories: residents of a particular area, parents of young children, university graduates, etc; all of these may be relevant in determining the response of 'the community' to a particular question, and they may not all pull in the same direction.

The second difficulty with community as the basis for collective action is the problem of holding everyone to what 'the community' believes to be the right thing to do, particularly when people have some incentive not to go along with the community. This is Hardin's 'tragedy of the commons': 'the community' may believe that the common should be husbanded so that everyone can use it, but each individual member of that community would benefit from exploiting it as an individual. The community may be opposed to shops trading on Sunday, but if one or two shops do open and get a lot of business, the other shops have to weigh their personal interest against the wishes of the community. For this reason, it is commonly argued that the clear wishes of the community should be backed up with law, with legal sanctions to prevent people flouting community values. Here we have an example of one model being invoked to correct the failure of another.

The focus on community as a basis for social action derived from our understanding of a pre-industrial world in which people had multiple-stranded, face-to-face relationships. But in urban industrial society, relationships are characteristically indirect and single stranded: we have single relationships with other people, for specific purposes. We may not interact with those people in any other context, and we may not even see them. In this anonymous, mass society there is less uniformity of beliefs and values across a larger group; relationships with more distant people are necessarily less intense; and the long-term accounting needed to keep track of obligations is more difficult the more people involved, and the more they come and go.

Finally, affiliation can act as the basis not of organisation but of dis-organisation. The legitimacy of organisational arrangements may be challenged or covertly undermined by a sense of community, which excludes as well as includes. It includes Protestants but excludes Catholics, for example, it includes whites but excludes blacks. The organisational structures of a state may be rejected in favour of those representing a more authentic 'community'. And the process can be repeated, as people challenge the newly recognised community, and seek to divide it into smaller and even more authentic communities, as happened in parts of the former USSR. The strength of people's attachment to their own community may be matched by their hostility to outsiders, and (particularly where attachment to the community is strong) communities may expel members whose commitment is regarded as suspect, or the community may break into smaller and even more intense communities.

Empirical Mixtures

The point here is not to find the one model of organisation which best describes real organisations: all organisations are, in a sense, alloys, combining elements of the different models, but in varying weights or combinations. As we saw earlier, teachers in universities tend to rely more on students' judgements about their self-interest to get them to class; secondary schools are more likely to use rules. This is not to say that school students do not feel that it is in their interest to attend class, or that university students do not feel any sense of obligation to attend classes. But identifying these three fundamental bases for organisation enables us to make comparisons – between these two organisations, or the same organisation at different times, or between different departments within the university.

A helpful analogy here is the primary colours – blue, yellow, red, etc. Most of the objects that we see do not match the primary colours exactly, but we use the primary colours to distinguish between the shades we see. 'Yes', we say to the sales person in the paint shop, 'I want some maroon paint, but not as red as that; something with a little more blue in it'. In the same way, we can see the differing ways that organisational arrangements can draw on norms, incentives and rules to get people to work together. The mix may be different in different times and places. In a school, for instance, the principal may be able to work mainly through relationships of hierarchical authority, but with the parents' association will probably rely much more on affiliation, on people seeing themselves as 'parents' and wanting to work together as a community with other people in that category.

Logical Interdependence

It is not simply that the models are found to be combined in practice: there is a sense in which they are logically linked to one another. Self-interested exchange relies on shared norms and values (so that they can trust one another enough to do deals) and external authority (so that the deals they make can be enforced if necessary). In the same way, the strength of authority rests on some recognition of the community to which that authority relates, and some broad sense that the existence of authority is in everyone's best interest. In this context some economists (e.g. Williamson) argue that the existence of hierarchy can be derived logically from the market model: it arises to meet those situations where market exchange would be more costly than bureaucratic rules, and in this sense bureaucracy can be explained as a market failure. But this is a logical argument rather than an empirical one: it is not claimed to be an account of what actually happened. So while there are links between the models we find it more analytically useful to keep them as three separate models than to try to reduce everything to one universal model of individual rationality.

Applying the Models to Cases

So far we have used hypothetical examples to illustrate our argument about organisation. Next we try out the models on three more realistic cases: youth homelessness, the epidemic of HIV/AIDS, and broadcasting. We have chosen these cases for several reasons.

First, they are currently regarded as important by politicians and the media in many industrial countries.

Second, each case involves complex interaction between public, private and voluntary organisations, rather than activity within a single organisation.

Third, these complex organisational arrangements are currently being questioned, for example in debates about the future of 'public service broadcasting', or of the role of housing associations in helping the homeless, or of community organisations in combating the spread of HIV/AIDS.

Fourth, while each is a 'public' problem it is also an issue that students often experience privately: facing problems with housing; being at risk of HIV/AIDS; and as consumers of broadcast radio and TV. This personal knowledge provides an alternative to official and media accounts.

We first analyse each case model by model, and then we step back and ask 'what does our analysis show about the process of organising?' We take a whole field of action, and identify and analyse the patterns of organisation that are found there. What are the patterns of organising that we find in relation to HIV/AIDS, or broadcasting, or youth homelessness? How do the participants draw on the possibilities open to them? And what alternatives would be possible?

By unpacking the organisation surrounding these 'problems' we hope to show that more is involved than a simple appeal for the government to do something, or do more. Governments are already involved, often in contradictory or indirect ways. They are often part of the problem, as well as part of the solution.

Review

1. 'Failure' refers to the circumstances in which the world fails to live up to the expectations of our models about it.
2. The sources of 'market failure' are:

   • monopoly (or the absence of competitors)
   • externalities (effects on neighbours or third parties)
   • lack of information
   • public goods (which can be enjoyed without being paid for).

3. The sources of 'bureaucratic failure' are:

   • disobedience and passive resistance
   • professional autonomy
   • segmentary organisation
   • inadequate information and time to decide.

4. The sources of community failure are:

   • overlapping and inconsistent membership
   • divergence between individual and community interests
   • urbanisation
   • exclusion and subdivision.

5. Actual organisations are mixtures of the three models.
6. The failure of one model may be corrected by another model.

Questions for Discussion

1. What examples of 'market failure' can you identify in each of the following examples?

- a weekend street market
- the defence industry
- the stock market
- secondary or tertiary education.

2. What examples of 'bureaucratic failure' can you identify in each of the following examples?

- a social security office
- a large private firm
- the army
- a school or university/college.

3. What examples of 'community failure' can you identify in each of the following examples?

- a family
- a network of friends
- a tribe
- a school or university/college.

4. To what extent could another model of organisation suggest remedies to each of the failures you have identified?

Further Reading

Ouchi (1980) works from 'market failures' to explain the existence of bureaucracies and what he calls 'clans'. He works in a tradition called 'markets and hierarchies', pioneered by Williamson (1975) and summarised in Williamson and Ouchi (1983) and Krusselberg (1986). Gretschmann (1986) discusses the relationship between what he calls 'solidarity' and markets. Atkinson and Coleman (1992: 162) argue that 'networks and communities are natural conceptual responses to both the limits of markets and hierarchical arrangements'.

5   Case Study 1: Youth Homelessness

The first of the policy areas to which we will apply an organisational perspective is youth homelessness. Youth homelessness has become a significant public policy issue for a number of countries in the 1990s. There has been widespread concern about the number of young people living on the streets because they have no home.

To what extent is this an organisational question? In one sense, it raises organisational questions because it is seen as an issue about which governments are expected to do things. But that category 'action by government' is part of a much broader question, 'how housing is organised', and in this chapter we will show how the policy issue of youth homelessness can be illuminated by asking organisational questions, and by applying our three models.

When something is said to be going wrong it is often helpful to start by clarifying how it goes normally. How is the housing of young people organised?

How Housing is Organised

People organise their housing in a number of ways, and our three models of organisation help us to understand the diversity of housing practice in industrial societies in the 1990s.

Market

There is, obviously, a housing market. Housing is a commodity which is bought and sold, and to a large extent this is seen as the 'normal' way to secure housing: you rent or buy the sort of housing that you like and that you can afford. Many people own their own housing, are in the process of buying it, or aspire to do so. Those who do not own housing rent it from other people, often with the intention of buying their own when they can afford it.

The existence of this market demand for housing encourages the supply. Entrepreneurs build houses and flats for sale or for rent, or they adapt existing buildings to current demand: large nineteenth-century houses, or warehouses, or wool stores, are divided into flats suitable for today's occupiers.

Bureaucracy

The main form of housing provision may be the market, but in most industrial countries a significant amount of housing is provided by public authority. Governments became involved in the provision of housing as a welfare activity because the sort of housing that the poor could afford to buy on the market was regarded as inadequate. Governments then established housing enterprises of their own, usually building accommodation and renting it to people who satisfied certain prescribed criteria.

These government housing operations are not so much an alternative to the market as a supplement to it. They are in any case market-like activities, in that rent is paid, but the rent is not necessarily a market rent, the enterprise is not expected to return a profit, and there has been a substantial inflow of government funds from the budget. But in recent years the trend has been for public housing to operate more on market lines, with rents aligned to market levels. There has also been a significant selling of public housing to existing occupants, particularly in the UK.

Community

The main organisational alternative to the market for the supply of housing is the community, of which the most relevant form is the family. For many people, housing is not something you have to buy or rent, but something that comes to you through your standing in a family. Most young people, and many older people, are housed in this way, at least for some of the time. The family represents a form of housing that people can fall back on if market provision is unavailable or unacceptable. Elements of market relationships may come into it, e.g. when a young person has a job but is still living in the family home, she may pay something for her board, but it is primarily seen as a family relation ship, not a market transaction.

People may also look to other sorts of community arrangements for answers to their housing needs. They may find a group of people whom they trust and with whom they feel comfortable, and seek housing together. Urban squatters would be a good example of people finding housing in this way. Young people, in particular, may draw on community relationships when other housing arrangements break down, 'crashing' with friends until they can work out something else.

Beyond the family and these sorts of 'housing community' there are also various forms of housing established and maintained by religious or ethnic groups for members of that community, such as senior citizens' homes. In other words, people may not only share their own housing with others with whom they feel some community affiliation, they may contribute to creating housing for people whom they may not know but who are members of that community. Again, there are market elements, in that there will be a charge made, but it will not necessarily be a 'market rate', nor will the enterprise be seeking a 'market return'.

Organising Housing for Young People

Given all this provision of housing, why is there a problem of youth homelessness? It is useful to work through our three organisational models: how do young people fare in each?

Beginning with the market, the young people who end up in the category 'homeless youth' tend not to have much money – whether capital to buy housing, or a regular income stream to enable them to rent it. So they often can't afford what the market offers, particularly as these offerings tend to be bigger packages than many young people want – a whole house or flat when they just want some space of their own. They may also find it difficult to produce the references from previous landlords, bankers or other authority figures that may be needed to secure rental housing. In other words, they find it difficult to meet their housing needs in the market-place.

But public authorities, we recall, became involved in housing precisely because some people could not afford what the market provided. Our young people would be likely to find, however, that these authorities were oriented to providing housing for families rather than single young people, and while they may have begun to change to accommodate the increasing number of young homeless, e.g. changing their rules of eligibility, the bulk of their housing stock is still of the 'family' type. And even though the rents they charge may not always be at market levels, they do still charge rents, and young people without regular income would have difficulty persuading the housing authorities that they could pay the rent regularly. So these young people may not find it easy to get housing through public authorities.

The third way of organising housing was community. As we saw, the primary community affiliation which provides housing is family ties. Young people concerned often report tension in their families as a result of which they 'have had to leave home'. There may be friction between young people and their parents. This is often aggravated by recent changes in the family; by an increasing rate of family breakdown; by separation, divorce, single-parent families, new partners, and often blended families. This means that for the young person the family may not represent stability and identity, but conflict and stress. There may be conflict with parents and step-parents (*de jure* and *de facto*), and the young person may decide to leave home.

For this young person there may be 'community' options, but they may be hard to find, and short term. They may be able to 'crash' with friends for a few days, but not for an indefinite period, particularly if they can't make a financial contribution. And the religious and ethnic groups providing housing tend to be oriented to old people rather than young people. So young people stepping outside the family may find it difficult to find another framework around which to organise their housing.

What is the Problem?

The existence of different ways of organising housing is not simply an interesting quirk of a diverse society. It is related to the different needs that people have (and their differing capacity to meet them) as they pass through the life cycle. Children are not expected to house themselves: it is expected that their housing will be provided through the community (i.e. the family). As they move from the dependence of childhood into the independence of adulthood they usually establish their own households, through the market or through the bureaucratic mode. As they move into old age, they may become more reliant on bureaucratic provision or the community.

This simplified presentation of the process has simply talked of the transition from dependence to independence. But this is a multi-stranded transition: there are several dimensions of dependence, and people move to independence at different rates on the different dimensions. The most important of these dimensions for our purposes are:

- citizenship: being entitled to take decisions for yourself
- labour market: being able to earn your own living
- housing: having your own accommodation.

As the transition from dependence to independence is a social construct, it is likely to be variable (i.e. it may be different in different spheres of life) and changing (i.e. young people may be regarded as more autonomous now than 20 years ago). So young people may find that they are regarded as competent guardians of their own interests in one sphere, but still subject to someone else's authority in another.

Moreover, their relative independence in terms of citizenship may be quite at variance with their continuing dependence in the labour market and the housing market. They may be full-time students with little income of their own, so that while they are legally independent, as far as the labour market is concerned, they remain dependent on their parents. They may be entitled to drive, but they still have to ask to borrow the car. And if they are not independent in the labour market they are probably not independent in the housing market either, and this may operate to limit the significance of their socio-legal independence: their legal right to engage in sexual relations is limited by having to share a bedroom with a younger brother or sister.

This means that youth itself is a complex, ambiguous and changing status, and this is likely to be reflected in the way that the housing of young people is organised.

One thing that is changing is the way in which the question is framed, and the implications of this for governmental action. Social values and practices in relation to young people and their housing are changing, which makes it likely that government will become more involved, both in the redefinition of the legal framework and in providing services which might have been previously left to the community (including the family) or market forces. For instance, a 14-year-old who leaves home without parental authorisation might once have been termed a 'runaway' child. Today, the same child might be described as 'homeless'. The implication of the first term is that the child ought to return home and official efforts should be directed to achieving this end. The implication of the second term is that the child should be provided with a home of his or her own, and the practical construction placed on this is that government should provide one.

In the second place, there are important changes in the nature of the labour market. Entry into the workforce is part of the movement to adult status. Traditionally, young people left school and went to work. The transitional status of young people in the workforce was recognised in various ways. One obvious way was the institution of apprenticeship, under which the young person worked for lower wages and continued to receive instruction, from the employer or an educational institution or both. And generally young workers were paid lower wages than older workers, quite likely too low a wage to sustain an independent household,

Changes both in the pattern of education and in the nature of the workforce have disrupted this assumption that education comes first and is followed by entry into the labour force. Education is taking much longer, as more young people stay on beyond the minimum school leaving age. More young people are continuing past school into tertiary education. And significant numbers of older people are returning to both secondary and tertiary education, often as part-time students.

At the same time there are significant changes in the nature of the workforce. The service industries have grown as a proportion of the economy, and along with this there has been an expansion in part-time employment, particularly among young people under the age of 18 (who are cheaper to employ). So there has been a substantial rise in part-time employment among young people, and a slight decline in full-time employment. And there has also been a significant rise in long-term unemployment among young people.

So there is less of a clear transition from education to work. Work is quite likely to start while the person is still in education, and finishing education may not mean beginning work. Young people may have attained most or all of their citizenship rights but because of prolonged education not be financially independent. They may be participating in the workforce, but in a marginal, low-paid and insecure status. This means that the extent to which young people are achieving independent status through workforce participation may be quite uneven.

Thirdly, there have been significant changes in the participation of young people in the housing market. The traditional model assumes a movement from living with the family (dependence) to setting up on one's own (independence), coinciding with the attainment of financial independence. But increased participation in education and changes in the nature of the labour market mean that for many young people financial independence may not be attained for some time.

These people are therefore in a weak position in the housing market, so there is a continuing reliance on the family as a source of housing. But as we have seen, the family itself is changing, and young people are less likely to look to the family for their housing needs. As the number of young people in this position grows there is a demand that governments should provide housing for these 'homeless children'.

'Youth Homelessness' as an Organisational Question

We can see that the problem of youth homelessness has to be understood in terms of 'housing' as an organised activity. We can identify a housing market, and identify the position of young people in it, but we can only really understand their position in the housing market in relation to (on the one hand) their position in relation to the labour market and citizenship, and (on the other) in relation to their access to non-market forms of housing, i.e the family and the government.

If all the dimensions of the transition to adulthood were synchronised with one another there would be less of an organisational problem. If everyone stayed at school until they were 18, did three years of full-time education while continuing to live at home, and at 21 got a job and established their own household, then the transition would be very neat and there would be no problem of youth homelessness. It is when these different dimensions of the transition are out of sync with one another that we see the strains, e.g. the young couple who continue to live with parents not because of their devotion to the family but because of necessity. The 16-year-old who leaves home after conflicts with parents (or step-parents) is another example of the strains that come from the different dimensions of the transition being out of sync: asserting citizenship rights, but without the labour market position to be able to afford appropriate accommodation on the housing market.

So it is important to take the organisational dimension into account when looking at policy questions. In this chapter we saw that the policy problem of youth homelessness was grounded in basic questions of social organisation: how is the transition from dependent to independent status managed, and what happens when some aspects of the transition proceed ahead of others? This is not a problem for an organisation, nor is it a problem of an organisation, but it is an organisational problem.

Similarly, the answer to the question of youth homelessness was seen to be framed by organisation. 'Market', 'hierarchy' and 'community' all implied distinct ways of organising the provision of housing, and each was evident, in different degrees, in the actual organisational arrangements. Changes in the nature of the family, in social values, in the structure of the workforce, in the agendas of governments, all affected the way in which young people could fit themselves into these organisational arrangements. The organisational dimension was not just a postscript to the solution but a part of both problem and solution.

Review

1. The policy question ('what should government do about youth homelessness?') is part of a broader organisational question ('how is housing organised?').
2. Housing is organised through the market (for sale or rent), though bureaucracy (public housing) or through community (family or friends).
3. Young people may be particularly disadvantaged by each form of organisation.
4. People are more reliant on some forms than others at different stages in their life cycle.
5. 'Youth' is transitional, involving changes in citizenship, labour market and housing status.
6. These changes in status are not well coordinated, and changes in family law, education and the workforce also affect the problem of 'youth homelessness'.

Questions for Discussion

1. Use the same framework to analyse the housing problems of old people, asking particularly:

   • how do the elderly fare within each form of organisation of housing?
   • what forms of housing predominate in the latter stages of people's life cycle?
   • to what extent is 'elderly' a transitional status?
   • what are the citizenship and labour market dimensions of being old, and how are these changing?

- to what extent do these changes impact on the problem of housing for older people?
- what is different about homelessness among young people and homelessness among older people, and what is similar?

2. Compare the problem of youth homelessness with problems of housing faced by ethnic or sexual minorities.

Further Reading

The Institute of Medicine (1988) and Caton (1990) summarise research on homelessness in the USA. Grago (1991) offers a critique of Australian policy towards homeless youth. Otherwise students should look for reports produced by and for different levels of government and voluntary agencies or lobby groups in their own country.

6 Case Study 2: Responding to the Epidemic of HIV/AIDS

This chapter uses the three models of organisation to analyse the response to the early stages of the epidemic of HIV/AIDS in industrialised countries. The epidemic is new and deadly. Worldwide, it is still in its early stages. So it should be a good test case for the view of organisation as collective problem solving discussed at the end of Chapter 2. In practice, reactions have also been shaped by memories of earlier epidemics, and by prejudices against the groups among whom it first appeared. So far, community level responses have been more successful than government programmes in slowing the spread of infection (Mann, 1992:4), and we pay particular attention to the 'community' model in this chapter.

The human immunodeficiency virus (HIV) causes illness both in itself and indirectly by weakening the body's immune system. People with HIV eventually become vulnerable to other infections, some of which can be treated, but others of which are fatal. No cure or vaccination has yet been found. HIV is transmitted through unprotected anal and vaginal sex, blood-to-blood contact (particularly needle sharing), and from mothers to babies before childbirth. Acquired Immune Deficiency Syndrome (AIDS) refers to the weakened state of the immune system, rather than the particular infections. The present group of people with AIDS are the leading edge of a much larger group of people with HIV.

In the US and other industrial countries the disease appeared mainly amongst gay men, injecting drug users and people with haemophilia. (In Africa and other developing countries it appeared more equally among men and women.) Gay men in industrial countries were relatively well organised as a community both to look after people who became sick and to slow the spread of infection among themselves. Injecting drug users were less well organised. Supplies of blood in industrial countries were so organised that they could be made safe after tests became available.

The early pattern of infection in industrial countries, and organisation around it, may change with increased heterosexual transmission, and transmission from mothers to babies. However, gay men still make up the largest group affected and we concentrate on them in order to demonstrate the interplay between the three models of organisation. We use the models to analyse the response, and we see how those involved used the models to persuade others to act.

Market

The market model assumes that people are the best judges of their own interests. But they need to be well informed about their choices, and able to calculate them. The publicity campaigns to limit the spread of HIV have also shown that people need to recognise themselves as at risk, demonstrating links with the community model, through issues of 'identity'.

Ignorance about methods of transmission characterised the early stages of the epidemic, and continues to affect some newspaper coverage and popular opinion. Many people became infected before the disease was discovered. The long period of incubation means that many people with HIV are unaware of the fact. Yet they can pass on the infection through sex involving body fluids, sharing needles in drug use or other kinds of blood-to-blood contact. Problems of informed choice continue to arise in debates about testing for HIV. The possibility of treatment using drugs such as Zidovudine (AZT) has provided a new incentive to get tested, but there are still good personal reasons to avoid acquiring the information. People become depressed at knowing they have an incurable and eventually fatal infection, and they may face discrimination at work and in housing if others know the result.

The free flow of information required by the market model can be frustrated in other ways. Knowledge of the disease is rapidly changing, and there can be genuine disagreements about what counts as a fact (for example, what exactly counts as 'safer sex'). The absence of symptoms also makes deception possible. People with HIV may be reluctant to tell their partners. And however truthful they may be, information campaigns face resistance from people who are suspicious of any information given by their employers or governments.

The association of the infection with homosexuality and drug use which may be illegal or regarded as shameful creates other problems of information. People may avoid testing or treatment to avoid imprisonment or damage to their reputation. Government officials, school teachers and doctors may be squeamish about providing information about safer ways of having sex or taking drugs.

The circumstances of transmission, during sex or drug use, also threaten the model of rational, calculating individualism underlying the market model. First, people may not act rationally about sex, and seem to be more likely to have unsafe sex if they are drunk, or in love. Second, they may not recognise themselves or their partners in information campaigns. There are psychological mechanisms of denial: 'it can't happen to me', or 'this person is so attractive, intelligent, well educated, etc that he or she cannot have HIV'. These denials may be aggravated by identification of the illness with stigmatised minorities, or different ethnic or racial groups.

Men having sex with men may not recognise themselves as 'gay', and so fail to respond to information targetted at 'gay men'. Gay rights activists argue that by 'coming out', and identifying with a visible gay community, gay men will receive social support for acting sensibly about sex in a time of AIDS, by choosing celibacy or monogamy with an uninfected partner, or by reducing the number of partners, limiting types of sexual activity and insisting on safe sex. In this sense membership of 'community' gives a person the information and self-confidence to make the rational choices that are a condition of the market model.

As the disease affects more and more women, treating people as undifferentiated 'individuals' may fail to capture relevant gender differences between them. Physiological differences between men and women affect the likelihood of transmission, and may affect the course of infection. Power differences within heterosexual relationships may make it more difficult for women than men to negotiate safe sex.

Community

Several levels or types of 'community' seem to be at work, sometimes at cross-purposes, in response to the epidemic. Each is quite fragile, and has been stressed as well as sustained by the epidemic. Each is potentially divided, and has to be mobilised and sustained by the action of its members (and the reactions of its critics and enemies).

Government campaigns distinguish a national community, and subnational communities associated with particular 'risk groups'. In the early stages of the epidemic many governments tried to close their borders against the virus by insisting on tests for migrants or other visitors. In later stages some governments have emphasised consensus and rejected discrimination within a presumed national community. Others also make their pitch to this national community. Members of threatened communities appeal for funds from the national budget, and warn of the consequences for the national community if it is withheld. Their opponents also appeal to a national audience when they invoke supposedly common norms and values against domestic minorities, or foreigners, or warn that national policy has been captured by a 'gay lobby'.

Another set of potential communities consists of those who have become ill, those with HIV, and those at risk. In the early spread of HIV in industrialised countries several categories of people were identified as 'at risk'. But categories of people do not necessarily form communities and the risk did not lie in membership itself but in particular acts of sex or needle sharing and the chances of contact with an infected person (for people with haemophilia it was exposure to a particular batch of infected blood).

Gay men were partly organised before the epidemic, through networks of friendship, around political campaigns, and around a largely commercial infrastructure of bars, saunas and other places where people met for sex or to start longer term relationships. Some people with haemophilia were formally organised in associations designed to represent their interests to the health care officials. Injecting drug users were minimally and more intermittently organised around the supply and use of drugs. There were differences in the forms and degree of organisation according to:

- which proportion of potential members they sought to include
- how much the organisations mattered to their members
- how long they lasted
- whether they were legal or illegal
- the extent to which their members could choose whether or not to become drug users, gay or haemophiliac.

The boundaries of these communities are not necessarily very clear. For example, the famous Kinsey report in the US identified a continuum between exclusively homosexual and exclusively heterosexual activity. No clear line could be drawn, and '37% of the total male population has at least some overt homosexual experience to the point of orgasm between adolescence and old age' (Kinsey et al, 1948: 650). More recent surveys suggest much lower figures. Some government campaigns distinguish between 'gay men' and 'men who have sex with men' but who do not necessarily identify with a gay community. Similarly, drug use may be casual or involve a substantial and exclusive commitment.

The response to HIV/AIDS shows how communities may be defined by exclusion, as well as inclusion. Much of the official discussion about HIV/AIDS among gay men and drug users concerns fear of its spread to 'the general community' (as if members of these minorities were not listening, or did not count). Exclusion, however, can provide the conditions for a counter-community, based on a sense of solidarity against shared victimisation.

Resistance to regulation is one of the defining characteristics of gay political organisations created to fight legal prohibitions against homosexuality or discrimination against gays and lesbians. (The pink triangle symbol of gay political activism, for example, refers back to the label on the uniforms used to distinguish homosexuals from other types of prisoner in Nazi concentration camps). Gay community groups have therefore tended to be suspicious of government initiatives that singled them out.

We can analyse and compare the attributes of these two claims to community – national and gay – along the several dimensions suggested by Taylor: common beliefs and values; direct many-sided relationships; reciprocity; threats of self-help retaliation; use of gossip, shaming and supernatural sanctions. A similar analysis could be applied to other communities organising around HIV/AIDS: religious groups; subcommunities of the gay community; and class, racial or ethnic communities that cut across them.

The epidemic has highlighted the absence of *common beliefs and values* about sexuality and drug use. Very few nation states include only one ethnic, linguistic, religious or racial group, and public health programmes in multicultural states have been tailored to meet groups' different expectations and sensitivities. The absence of common beliefs and values within and between groups affected, or at risk, also limits the possibilities for mobilising around community forms of organisation.

National communities are mostly too large to sustain *direct many-sided relationships* among their citizens. Visibility and geographical proximity become important in determining the possibilities of reciprocity among affected subnational communities. Among married or bisexual men, or men in country areas, this condition of community with other gay men is absent. The only connection may be through sex. The geographic dispersal of other categories of people at risk, such as people with haemophilia, makes organising themselves into a community more difficult.

National communities are also too large to provide opportunities for *reciprocity* except of the most generalised kind, expressed perhaps through welfare systems. The identification of the disease with stigmatised minorities prevents members of the majority seeing that 'it might happen to me.' Some degree of identification or empathy seems necessary for reciprocity. Gay community organisations now provide support groups, 'buddy' systems to look after people who have become sick, and information lines based on reciprocity.

Self-help retaliation operates at both levels of community. Members of national communities sometimes claim that overriding reasons of public health allow them to 'take the law into their own hands' and exclude or evict people suspected of infection. National governments are often tempted to take unilateral action, for example against immigrants, in spite of international agreements. And the rise in 'gay bashing' in inner-city suburbs has led some gay communities to organise defensive networks, and to institutionalise links with the police to ensure that cases are reported and followed up.

Finally, *gossip, shaming and supernatural sanctions* sustain each level of community. The tabloid press sustains a sense of national community by gossip and shaming, for example in stories about pop and film stars suspected of 'having AIDS'. Right-wing politicians and religious leaders see the work of supernatural sanctions in the epidemic, punishing the deviant and saving the community of the respectable. Among affected minorities, gossip and shaming can be invoked against people who continue with unsafe sex, or needle sharing.

Bureaucracy

A bureaucratic approach emphasises rules, for example compulsory HIV testing or quarantine for people with the illness or the virus, or simply suspected of being at risk. Such rules are easier to invoke against already regulated populations: immigrants, prisoners, indigenous minorities, schoolchildren or the military. Nevertheless, responses to HIV/AIDS have provided numerous examples of failures of hierarchy and rules. Applying Hood's model of 'perfect administration' to government responses to HIV/AIDS we find the following.

1. An absence of *unitary organisation*, with agencies frequently at cross-purposes. When homosexuality or drug use are illegal, agencies trying to limit the spread of HIV among gay men or drug users often find themselves at cross-purposes with the police. Rights to privacy, or

against discrimination, have often conflicted with proposals for HIV testing.

2. A lack of *uniformity of norms and values* has been demonstrated in at least four ways. First, as discussed in relation to 'community' there are widely different norms and values about sexuality. Second, there are also norms of silence, and visibility: activities have often been tolerated, provided they are not talked about in public, where both men and women are present, or children. These norms make it difficult for educators to be specific (for example) about unprotected anal intercourse as an unsafe form of sex. Third, professional norms of doctors have sometimes come into conflict with government rules over, for example, notification of partners, or government officials, about people with HIV or AIDS. Fourth, the international character of the epidemic, and the role of international organisations in combating it, has created many opportunities for cross-cultural misunderstanding and taking offence.

3. Third, there has been a lack of *perfect obedience* among lower level officials charged with implementing policy, and among their clients, for example in reporting cases of infection.

4. Governments have typically acted without *full information* about the nature of HIV, the extent of the epidemic, or the sexual behaviour of the population. In the early stages of the epidemic some governments actively suppressed information for fear of its effects on the country's reputation. Assumptions about sexual behaviour tended to refer back to the 1948 Kinsey report about white American men. Drugs against HIV have tended to be tested on men rather than women, so information about particular effects of women's physiology is not being gathered.

5. Governments have often not given themselves adequate *time to consider* responses. Typically, they have ignored the unpleasant evidence and then overreacted to a media-induced panic.

In any case, homosexual activity, prostitution and drug use are illegal in many jurisdictions where HIV/AIDS is spreading. Stronger rules, or stronger enforcement of existing rules may be not only ineffective, but counterproductive, driving people underground.

Rules may also interfere with community or market-oriented approaches to limiting the spread of HIV, such as advertising condoms, or making them available with less embarrassment through vending machines. But they do not have to be made by governments: the Sydney gay newspaper *Campaign* publishes a set of rules for people wanting to advertise for partners in its personal columns. These include: 'Terms like "AIDS-free", "HIV negative" and similar are out. There is no way of knowing if such claims are genuine, even if based on a recent test result.'

Conclusions

The response to the epidemic shows that organising is not simply a matter of designing the new structures to achieve an agreed common purpose. Organisations are already in place, with their own turf to protect and interests to promote, and their members may have quite divergent purposes.

Recognition of the existence of the disease itself depended on organisational factors. In a decentralised, mainly privately funded health system like that in the US, individual diagnoses of particular patients had to be assembled into the picture of a national epidemic. Doctors began treating individual patients in different US cities for rare illnesses in the early 1980s. Though they may have been puzzled by particular cases, they had no picture of an underlying 'problem' expressed in these individual illnesses. It was first defined by epidemiologists at the Centers for Disease Control who looked for causes in the 'lifestyle' of 'risk groups', particularly gay men. Once a virus was identified a different group of specialists redefined the problem in terms of infection susceptible to vaccines and drugs. Talk about 'risk groups' partly gave way to talk about 'risky activities', like unprotected sex and needle sharing (Oppenheimer, 1992: 63–64).

In countries with more centralised health systems, or less well-organised communities of people affected, the response has been different. And in poorer countries the statistics have been less available, and the epidemic less visible against a background of other signs of poor health. Resources have been less available for government information campaigns or publicly funded hospital treatments. Poorer countries thus choose 'community' and preventive approaches by default: neither their national health budgets nor the private incomes of most of their citizens, can afford expensive treatments for the infections to which people with AIDS succumb.

In addition to their use in analysis of the early epidemic among risk groups, the models can be used to consider organisation as the epidemic spreads more widely through heterosexual and perinatal transmission.

Perhaps the biggest organisational change will involve use of the 'community' model.

The early response in western countries relied heavily on organisations set up mainly by gay men, which in turn relied on social and political networks built up during campaigns for law reform. Community responses were facilitated by the geographical concentration of populations initially affected and by their abililty to make links to governments. As the epidemic spreads more widely among less, or differently, organised groups the response may require greater use of (on the one hand) bureaucratic rules and (on the other) appeals to individual self-interest. Ethnic or indigenous groups may already define themselves as communities in ways that facilitate, or inhibit, transmission of information. 'Community' responses may become more difficult as the categories of people affected become broader and their number grows.

The case also shows how models of community, hierarchy and the market are called on to mobilise support for policy proposals. Conservative groups appeal to supposed community norms and values against sexual promiscuity, or homosexuality. Community groups like the AIDS Coalition to Unleash Power (ACT UP) call on governments to change the rules governing new drug treatments or eligibility for sickness benefits. The World Health Organisation calls on governments to educate their populations about the risks.

The organisation of the response to the epidemic shows how each model cannot simply be judged on grounds of its 'effectiveness' (in spite of the tendency to use military metaphors of 'fighting disease', Sontag, 1989: 11). In each case there are moral overtones to the preference for one kind of organising over another. Communities are, after all, defined in terms of norms and values embraced by members and rejected by non-members. Some people distinguish 'innocent' from presumably 'guilty' sufferers who caught the virus through sexual contact. Often there is a strong urge to punish behind proposals for tougher rules against the spread of infection. Values of individual autonomy underlie proposals for more market-oriented responses to the epidemic. And values of solidarity underlie community responses.

Review

1. Gay men, injecting drug users and people with haemophilia were differently organised when HIV/AIDS emerged first among them.

2. Different organisational questions arise when the disease spreads through heterosexual transmission, and from mothers to babies.
3. The market model relies on people acting in their own self-interest to avoid infection.
4. In the early stages of the epidemic in industrial countries there were difficulties with relying on self-interest because of:

    • ignorance about the cause and methods of transmission
    • lack of symptoms among people infected
    • reasons to avoid finding out if you were infected
    • irrational behaviour associated with sex and drug use
    • people not recognising they were at risk.

5. The community model relies on changing norms and values about sex and drug use.
6. In the early stages of the epidemic in industrial countries there were difficulties in relying on community:

    • gay men were well organised as a community, but injecting drug users were less so
    • the boundaries of these communities were not very clear and did not necessarily include all those at risk
    • the gay community had a history of resistance to being singled out and discriminated against by governments
    • identification of the disease with minority communities allowed members of majority communities to become complacent about the spread of infection to them.

7. The bureaucratic model relies on rules about sex and drug use.
8. In the early stages of the epidemic in industrial countries there were difficulties in relying on rules:

    • organisations working at cross-purposes
    • different norms and values
    • imperfect obedience
    • lack of information
    • inadequate time to respond
    • interference between rules and community- or market-oriented responses.

9. Organisational factors, including the centralisation of health systems, affected the way the disease was first recognised.
10. Community, bureaucratic and market models of organisation are used by reformers proposing changes to HIV/AIDS policy.
11. The case shows the limits of a rational, instrumental approach that assumes people will act together to solve common problems.

Questions for Discussion

1. How would the response to HIV/AIDS in industrialised countries have differed if it had first emerged:

   - mainly among heterosexuals?
   - mainly among women?
   - mainly among ethnic minorities rather than white men?
   - in the 1950s rather than the 1980s?

2. How would the organisational response to HIV/AIDS have differed if:

   - a cure had been rapidly found?
   - a vaccination had been rapidly found?

3. Analyse the pattern of organising surrounding other sexually transmitted diseases.
4. To what extent, and why, is the pattern of organising in response to HIV/AIDS different in developing countries, compared with industrialised countries?
5. If heterosexual and mother-to-baby transmission become more significant in industrial countries what changes may become necessary to forms of organisation established in the early stages of the epidemic?
6. How might the three models of organisation help you design a campaign to limit the spread of HIV/AIDS among students?

Further Reading

For an authoritative global survey of the epidemic see Mann et al, eds. (1992). For the political philosophical issues arising in the US see Bayer

(1989). For changing constructions of the problem by different groups of scientists see Oppenheimer (1992). For different national policies in a number of industrialised countries see Kirp and Bayer, eds (1992), and comparing Britain and Germany see Freeman (1992). For the ambivalent relationship between HIV/AIDS and the gay community see Altman (1988 and 1991), Watney (1987) and Padgug and Oppenheimer (1992). For a critique of the 'Aids Service Industry' and issues of community, identity, race and class see Patton (1990: 5–23). For the relationship between state and community in relation to AIDS see Sears (1992: 66–68).

7   Case Study 3: Broadcasting

Broadcasting – including radio and TV – is a large and diverse world. It does not rest on a single organisation but on a web of organisation that allows the various individuals and public, private and voluntary institutions to pursue their own purposes. Broadcasting seems to call for a relatively high level of organising. Newspapers, by contrast, seem to require less. If you want to start a newspaper, you can do so whether it is in order to make money, to foster a sense of local identity, to promote a cause, to provide a vehicle for advertisements, or some combination of these. It is then up to you to get enough support, from readers, advertisers or sponsors, to keep the enterprise going. In other words, the dominant organisational form seems to be the market.

But broadcasting seems to be more regulated: there are licences, government broadcasters, and generally more governmental involvement. Two special features about broadcasting perhaps encourage organisation: one is the question of access to the spectrum; the other is the fact that broadcasting is a form of public good. These special features of broadcasting make sense of the quite complex organisational arrangements through which it is accomplished.

Technically, 'broadcasting' means disseminating messages by means of the radio spectrum; this includes radio, of course, and television, but also such things as radar, and point-to-point communications like citizens' band (CB) radio, or the networks used by the police or taxis. All of these need to have access to the radio spectrum – and here lies a particular problem for the administration of broadcasting: the different users don't just want access to the radio spectrum, they want exclusive use of some part of it. This is because simultaneous use of the same part of the spectrum causes mutual interference. If the airport radar and the radio-controlled taxis are both trying to use the same portion of the spectrum the result is unsatisfactory for both of them. In the same way, if two radio stations are broadcasting too close to one another on the spectrum they may both find that their listeners complain of poor reception.

The second distinctive feature of broadcasting that generates a demand for organisation is the fact that what is broadcast is essentially a form of common property to which anyone with the right type of radio (or TV set) has access. This means that it is difficult to charge people directly for using it. Broadcasting is, in fact, a classical illustration of what economists call a public good: if I have a radio, you cannot prevent me listening (non-excludable) and my enjoyment of the broadcast does not interfere with anyone else's enjoyment (non-rivalrous). It is a public good whether it is provided by government or a private company or a community group, and this immediately raises the question of how it is to be paid for. If you cannot prevent people who have not paid the charge from receiving the service, and everyone free rides, how is the service to be paid for?

Organising Access to the Spectrum

So we can start our investigation into the organising of broadcasting by thinking of the way access to the spectrum is organised. Here, different sorts of organising are possible, and it is helpful to use our three models of organising to clarify this. It is quite possible, for instance, to envisage the use of the radio spectrum being governed by the mobilisation of community values. After all, crowding may affect our enjoyment of the beach, just as it can interfere with our enjoyment of the air waves, but there is no tribunal to regulate our access to the beach, and no police on duty to arbitrate disputes between users. Beach users rely on shared perceptions of personal space, and on various ways (subtle and unsubtle) that people have of communicating to one another their expectations about how everyone should behave in this shared space. Surely it should be possible for people using community norms and processes to find adequate space for all the claimants on the radio spectrum? Amateur users of radio, for example, have developed a complex set of norms and values about appropriate use of the spectrum: about appropriate and inappropriate topics of conversation, about breaking into conversations, and closing them, and about giving priority to emergency uses. Citizens' band radio similarly developed its own community language and conventions.

Alternatively, we might expect to see the ordering of positions on the spectrum achieved by the working of market exchange. Broadcasters all have an interest in being heard by their audience. If the broadcasting from your radio station is interfering with the reception of my station it is in my interest to do a deal with you to eliminate the interference, and if the interference is mutual you have the same interest in doing a deal with me. Perhaps I might pay you to shift to a different frequency, or to broadcast on a more sophisticated transmitter that does not cause interference. The interference your station is causing is referred to by economists as an externality – one of your production costs that is carried by somebody else. But while in theory externalities might be carried by other parties, in the real world of business, enterprises will try to sheet them home to their source, and the law helps them.

If what you do in your business interferes with the running of my business (e.g. if you start a glue factory next to my hamburger shop), I may be able to take legal action to restrain you or to seek compensation. So if I had started broadcasting first and you had come along later, I can take legal action to prevent your interfering with my reception. The existence of this option of legal action may give us both an incentive to reach an agreement rather than face an expensive court case the outcome of which is uncertain.

The third possible way of organising the use of the spectrum is by the use of authority. People could look to the government, or some body acting with the authority of the government, to make an authoritative allocation among users of the spectrum band. This might involve two stages: first, a division among alternative uses, e.g. TV, radio and other uses of the band; and secondly, achieving separation between competing users, i.e. to prevent your radio station causing interference to mine. Making an allocation between uses may also involve making choices about technology, e.g. what provision is made for FM radio, or whether the TV sound channel should be carried on VHF or UHF. These have enormous implications for the manufacturers and repairers of equipment. Here, commercial suppliers may prefer to have a bureaucratic rule and a single system rather than competition between systems, as happened with video cassette recorders (VCRs) with the higher level of costs which that implies.

We can see that our three models offer three different ways of organising the use of the radio spectrum, and only one of them, the 'bureaucratic' model, involves setting up a clearly defined 'organisation'. It is important to bear this in mind, because the bureaucratic allocation of positions in the spectrum is the normal practice throughout the world, and it is easy to slip into the assumption that this is the way that it 'has to be'. By using our analytic models we can see that alternatives are possible, and that the use of the bureaucratic model is a significant element in the organising of broadcasting.

Organising a Public Good

In the same way, by using our models we can see alternative ways of handling the problem of broadcasting as a public good. Here, the question is how the service is to be paid for when people can enjoy it whether or not they've paid for it.

This is a particular problem for the market model, which relies on the market price not simply to pay for the service but also to establish the value, e.g. how much are people prepared to pay for improvements in quality? There are essentially two responses to this problem within the market model: finding ways to exclude non-payers, and finding new categories of payer.

Non-payers can be excluded through technological innovations which enable the broadcaster to limit reception to particular receivers (who can then be charged for the service). In the early days of radio there were 'sealed sets' which could receive only one station. Now it is possible to transmit a scrambled signal which can only be decoded by a special device attached to the receiver (and which has to be hired from the broadcaster). A similar development has been the introduction of cable TV, where the signal is transmitted by cable to the houses of subscribers. Strictly speaking, this is no longer broadcasting, but it has developed from broadcasting as a way of solving this problem of being a public good. In some countries it is possible to receive the programmes of the major networks either broadcast (for free) or by cable (better quality picture, for a fee).

The other response is to find new categories of payer by selling time within the broadcast to people who have a message they would like the broadcast audience to hear – in other words to add advertising to the broadcast. What this means, of course, is that the nature of the product itself is transformed: it is something in itself (say, a TV broadcast of a football match), and it is also a vehicle for advertising. And so there are two sorts of user: the viewer (who wants to watch the football) and the advertiser (who wants to catch the attention of the viewer). It is hard to exclude the first user but easy to exclude the second, so charging the second group of users becomes the way to finance the broadcast.

While there are market responses to the problem of public goods, the most common response lies within the authority model: if it's a public good, then the government ought to provide it. Street lighting, for instance, is available to everyone using the street, and so it is difficult to charge the users and it is seen as appropriate for some level of government to provide it. Governments are not dependent on being able to charge a price to the user: they can exact a contribution, whether in the form of a licence fee payable by users or in the form of taxation paid by everyone whether or not they are users. So governments can finance broadcasting and make it available to everyone. (How this might be done, and how directly the government would be involved in the service, would be another matter.)

Finally, another way of providing public goods is through the community model – that is, through people's sense of obligation to the other members of some group of which they are a part. If public goods cannot be provided by entrepreneurs because the cost cannot be recouped through market prices, they can be provided by benefactors who wish to give something to the community and are not looking for an economic return. Once such benefactors would have been wealthy individuals, but they could also be groups, ranging from well-defined groups like service clubs to large, relatively amorphous communal rallies like the Clean Up Australia campaign (which mobilised volunteers to clean up Sydney Harbour and other waterside locations).

Providing public goods through private benefactors (individual or collective) may be relatively uncommon, but it is clearly possible, and as governments at all levels respond to increasing financial stringency the idea of private sponsors for public benefits becomes increasingly attractive. Some Californian roads, for instance, now carry a sign indicating that the removal of roadside litter for the next two miles is the responsibility of some named sponsor, which might be a local business, a service club or a scout troop. The local business is interested in advertising itself, of course, but it is doing this by demonstrating its commitment to the welfare of the community, and along with the service club and the scout troop, offering another way to provide a public good.

So broadcasting might be financed by voluntary contributions motivated by a sense of obligation to the community. These might come from individuals or companies or non-profit organisations. The 'community' in question might be the community at large, or a local community, or an ethnic community.

Models and Sectors

In practice, broadcasting usually involves a mixture of methods of organising, and there is no simple identification of models with sectors. The relationship between state-owned broadcasters and government ministers, for example, is often not completely or successfully hierarchic.

The broadcasters may supplement their grant or licence revenue with commercial sponsorship, or revenue gained from the sale of their products. They may compete aggressively with commercial stations for audience share. They may contract out their programming, and compete with commercial stations for the rights to broadcast sporting events. Even the formally hierarchic aspects of their organisation may be subject to resistance and failure. Many countries have rules that require that state-owned broadcasters act autonomously of the government, particularly at election time. They may successfully resist ministers who try to impose rules about what they may broadcast. Similarly, the internal organisation of broadcasters often contradicts the hierarchic picture presented by organisation charts. Journalists, for example, have developed codes of professional ethics that often pit them against producers enforcing rules from above.

Just as state-owned broadcasting is not entirely rule driven, commercial broadcasting is not entirely the domain of the market. Privately owned broadcasters may take on 'public service' obligations in exchange for government protection against competition in the region they serve. They may be subject to government regulation about children's programmes, news and local content. They may also regulate themselves, without government prompting, over matters such as the number of advertisements, or the amount of violence they broadcast. Journalists' professional norms also cause them to resist pressures from shareholders and advertisers.

Finally, community-based broadcasting will often supplement its revenue by accepting commercial sponsorship while receiving indirect support from the government through tax deductions for voluntary contributions.

Interaction Between the Models

We have seen how the three models of organisation suggest different responses to problems of broadcasting: access to the spectrum and its character as a public good. The field of broadcasting also shows how each model deals with some circumstances better than others, and how one model may be invoked to deal with the 'failure' of another. In each case the replacement of one model with another is a matter of degree – a nudge in the direction of more markets, more hierarchy or more community.

We have also seen how broadcasting is characterised by what are often called 'market failures': the existence of an externality (interference) and its character as a public good (the technical problem of excluding non-payers). These market failures seem to justify government or community forms of regulation of broadcasting. But as we saw in Chapter 4, 'bureaucracy' and 'community' may fail too. Broadcasting provides several examples.

Bureaucratic Failure

Governments allocate bands of the spectrum to different uses, and licence particular users to operate at particular frequencies. This process demonstrates some of the limits of administrative rules.

First, the rules are inflexible. Officials are not necessarily good at anticipating demand, so parts of the spectrum may end up heavily used while others remain empty, and new types of use (such as mobile phones) are not anticipated. Governments typically look after themselves first, and large parts of the spectrum are allocated to military uses. Reallocation of frequencies is technically easy but becomes politically difficult as those already allocated space seek to hold on to it. Those advantaged in the present allocation – government departments or private operators – find it worthwhile to spend money in lobbying and litigation to protect their advantages.

Second, technical standards may have unexpected economic outcomes. They may serve as a way of protecting local manufacturers of equipment against cheaper imports that would benefit consumers. They may discourage innovation as manufacturers design products that meet, but do not exceed, the official standards. More generally they prevent users choosing to trade-off technical standards in exchange for other benefits, such as cheaper equipment or more channels.

Thirdly, rules are often ambiguous, inviting expensive litigation about, for example, which programmes count towards 'local content' or 'children's programming' rules.

Fourthly, rights to the spectrum have typically been allocated for free, or at prices that reflect administrative costs, rather than according to the scarcity value of the resource. Licences, in brief, have been worth far more to licensees than the amount government recovers from them (a British television company owner described his as a 'licence to print money'). The value of these licences becomes particularly visible if they can be bought and sold, but also shows up in the valuation of the assets of the companies that own them. What politicians condemn as 'windfall profits' economists describe as 'rent', which is the return in excess of that needed to encourage people to enter the market and provide the service.

Fifthly, there are economic costs involved in enforcing the rules, and these costs may not be sheeted home on the beneficiaries: general taxpayers, for example, pay the cost of administering licences that are worth millions of dollars to broadcasters.

These deficiencies in government regulation have led to proposals for 'more markets' in broadcasting. The British government now auctions TV licenses, offering them (with some conditions) to the highest bidder, thus recovering some of the 'economic rent' for taxpayers. New Zealand has privatised the spectrum, creating property rights that can be bought and sold. The aim is to use prices to encourage more efficient use of the spectrum. Frequencies in high demand will command higher prices than those in low demand. But these new forms of market organisation come with their own characteristic failures (discussed in Chapter 4).

Community Failure

Broadcasting reaches huge numbers of people from a single central point. It is thus a powerful instrument for imposing community values, from a centre to a periphery, or from a majority community (which owns a radio station) to a minority community (which does not). Programmes offered by state-owned broadcasters may reflect the norms and values of the ruling elites, even if these do bore or offend the powerless (the race, gender and accent of TV presenters are a good index of the dominant community style). In reaction, representatives of peripheral or minority communities may get governments to enforce rules requiring the use of local languages or other local content in programmes. Women, or ethnic, linguistic, religious and sexual minorities may lobby to ensure their images are represented in mainstream media, or demand channels of their own. Multilingual and multi-ethnic states typically have several broadcasters, and complex rules and conventions about who can broadcast what to whom. Typically these rules are enforced by granting, or denying, access to the spectrum.

Broadcasting as an Organised World

We can see, then, that broadcasting does not just happen: it has to be organised. Or to be more precise, while it is possible to imagine a libertarian world in which there were no restraints on broadcasting, we find that in practice there is always a pattern of ordered arrangements, which in some way rests on state authority. There seem to be no instances of access to broadcasting being determined by market exchange (even in the US, despite the widely shared faith in the market and a corresponding antipathy to 'government regulation'). The ordering of broadcasting seems to rely on authoritative rule making.

To say that 'state authority' is involved in the structuring of broadcasting is not to say that it is government controlled. Governments are involved in broadcasting in many different ways. In some countries they simply create mechanisms for others to get access to the airwaves. In others they become involved in the provision of broadcasting, through the creation and maintenance of official broadcasting agencies. Sometimes these agencies have a monopoly of broadcasting; more often, they take their place alongside other broadcasters, which may be commercial enterprises or non-profit operations. Even where the government has established an 'official' broadcaster it may or may not want this to be seen as a government activity: in the UK it is always made clear that the government does not run or control the BBC, whereas in France the official broadcaster is much more closely identified with the government.

So to some extent, the organising of broadcasting rests on the capacity of governments to make rules and provide services – in other words, the mobilisation of authority – but it also relies on some of the assumptions and practices of market exchange. Broadcasters are selling something: to the audience they are selling entertainment, to the advertisers they are selling an audience. Even non-commercial broadcasters may need to justify their activities in terms of the audience that they reach. To the extent that there are several broadcasters all trying to reach the same audience the organisation of broadcasting draws on the market model.

But it is not a free market, in that the competition is between only a select group of authorised providers: those who have been allocated a place on the spectrum. Here, we can see the organisation of broadcasting drawing from the market model the notion of property rights. A place on the spectrum from which you can broadcast without interference is (at least potentially) a valuable possession. State regulation of access to the spectrum guarantees the rights of those who are in there broadcasting. And if the people who are broadcasting are able to sell the right to do so to someone else, then their officially allocated position on the spectrum has become a form of property, and anyone who wants to enter broadcasting can do so only by buying the licence of an existing broadcaster.

But while spectrum allocation may lead to the establishment of individual property rights, and market trading, we can also see in broadcasting the assertion of collective property rights, and of shared values – in other words, people also draw on the concept of community. It can be argued that the airwaves are collective property, and that a broadcaster's access to them is subject to community norms – about decency, for instance, and fairness. So while a broadcast may be acceptable to the audience at which it is directed, others may be find it to be in breach of 'community standards'. The broadcaster has to have one eye on the market and the other on 'community standards', particularly in so far as they are expressed through bureaucratic rules.

We can see why the organisation of broadcasting is both complex and ambiguous: it draws simultaneously on all three of our models of organisation, and they may work against one another. The regulatory body may be discouraged from issuing new licences because it fears this may threaten the commercial viability of existing licensees. The order is always subject to variation and change. As community values change there may be consequent changes in the order of broadcasting, e.g. greater acceptance of ethnic minorities may lead to the emergence of ethnic broadcasting stations. Technological change also has an impact: the introduction of FM radio in Australia enabled the admission of new broadcasters without any need to disrupt the existing arrangements. And there is always the possibility of other broadcasting systems having an impact, as happened when the BBC monopoly in the UK was challenged by broadcasts from Europe and from 'pirate' broadcasters.

Broadcasting, then, rests on an organisational order which is the work of many hands, who may have different rationales for action. The end result may be described as 'government regulation' and explained as the consequence of policy goals, but a more careful analysis will show the complexity of the pattern.

Review

1. Broadcasting seems to be more subject to government regulation than other media.

2. Broadcasters need exclusive access to part of the radio frequency spectrum.
3. Broadcast information is also like a public good in the sense that it is non-rivalrous, and not easily excludable.
4. Broadcasting could be organised through each of the three models.
5. Broadcasting's character as a public good can be modified by excluding non-subscribers, and by charging advertisers, by compulsory taxation, by private benefaction or by mobilisation of community norms and values.
6. There is no simple identification between forms of organisation and public, private and community sectors of broadcasting: each shows a mix of models.
7. Broadcasting demonstrates examples of bureaucratic, community and market 'failure'.
8. The failures of one model are often corrected by bringing in another (e.g. taxation to fund public good provision).
9. Governments are deeply involved in broadcasting, but not simply to enforce rules.
10. Commercial broadcasters have to keep an eye on community standards.

Questions for Discussion

1. How is the pattern of organisation of broadcasting likely to be affected by the introduction of new technologies such as the following?

   • cable
   • direct satellite broadcasting.

2. How are changing community norms affecting the pattern of organisation of broadcasting in industrial countries?
3. How would the three models of organisation help you design the organisation of a student-run TV station?
4. Use the three models to analyse the pattern of organisation in non-broadcast media, such as:

   • books
   • videos
   • compact discs.

Further Reading

Leblebici et al (1991) analyse US broadcasting, and Veljanovski (1989) analyses UK broadcasting in organisational terms. Otherwise students should refer to government reports on the future of broadcasting in their own countries.

8   Models and Sectors

So far we have been talking about *the* organisation, but in the real world we encounter lots of different organisations, sometimes linked to one another, sometimes not, sometimes doing different things, sometimes doing the same thing. How can we make sense of this profusion of organisations, and do our models help?

We can identify three approaches to this question that might be helpful. One divides the organisational world into sectors, each with distinctive characteristics and modes of operation. The second approach accepts this division into sectors but has its focus on the links between the sectors. The third approach sees the organisational world as full of overlap and ambiguity, and looks for ways to clarify it through analysis.

Organisations and Sectors

One of the most common ways of making sense of the multiplicity of organisations is to divide them into sectors: the public sector, the private sector and, increasingly, the 'community sector' or 'third sector'. In many ways this looks like a mobilisation of our three models to sort out the world: there is a public sector organised on the basis of bureaucratic authority, a private sector organised on the basis of self-interested exchange, and a community sector organised on the basis of affiliation.

However, the three models were introduced not as descriptions of actual organisations but as abstract constructs which help us to clarify what is going on in organisations. Can they be used as sorting boxes to categorise actual organisations? Let us consider this question for each of the sectors.

The Public Sector

It is easy to see why the public sector is equated with bureaucratic authority. In the first place, the public sector is clothed with the symbols

73

of authority: even the buses and the letter boxes are likely to carry a coat of arms or logo. And the public sector is hierarchical in its own organisation: public bodies are established to give effect to the decisions of authorised leaders, and do this through a hierarchy of command. Finally, it stands in a hierarchical relationship to society: public bodies frame and execute rules which are then imposed on everyone else.

This presentation of the public sector is persuasive, but on closer examination doubts are raised. To some extent, the public sector seems to be structured as hierarchy based on authorised direction – ministers do exercise authority over their departments – but the exceptions are many, and important. Public service departments may be hierarchically subordinate to the government, but courts and tribunals are usually not. Some parts of the public sector are set up with their own governing bodies, whose members are generally drawn from outside government (often to represent particular interests) and are to a greater or lesser extent autonomous of the government. Universities may be created by governments but they are not instruments of government. And although local councils are set up by the government the extent to which they are subordinate to it is often debatable and may end up being tested in court.

And while we talk of 'the government' as a whole, we find that the term covers a wide range of functionally specialised organisations, each dealing with, for example, roads, fisheries, health or town planning. So perhaps 'the government' should be seen not as a hierarchy but as a collection of parallel hierarchies constitutionally independent of one another but linked by 'working relationships' between the participants. Officials working in one hierarchy will need to construct 'horizontal' relationships with their counterparts in other hierarchies. Officials running a hospital may have to deal with officials in town planning, education, roads, environmental protection, etc – not through the exercise of hierarchical authority but through discussion and agreement.

These 'horizontal' relationships are not confined within the public sector either. The hospital officials will have working relationships with doctors' organisations, unions, insurance companies and other bodies outside the public sector. These horizontal linkages create a loose organisational form brought together by a common interest in the particular field, an organisational form which has been termed 'the policy community'. It is based not on hierarchical authority but on overlapping concerns and a common interest in bringing about coordinated action.

And while we see government as having a hierarchical relationship with the rest of society – giving orders, making rules etc – governments seem to try to avoid relying on hierarchical authority. Max Weber's classic definition speaks of the state as having a monopoly of the legitimate use of violence, but empirical research suggests that there is a widespread preference in the public sector for avoiding coercion. Rules are framed after consultation with those affected by them, and organisations representing affected groups are drawn into the decision-making process. Their interests are recognised and accommodated, and governments sometimes pay compensation to those adversely affected by the exercise of government authority, i.e. hierarchy is supplemented by market exchange.

So while hierarchical authority is important in the organising of public bodies, the public sector cannot be equated with public authority. There is more to the public sector than hierarchy (and, it should be added, hierarchy is not confined to the public sector).

The Private Sector

People tend to see market relations as characteristic of the private sector: business enterprises survive or perish according to their ability to make successful market exchanges. But it is easy to overlook the extent that 'doing business' involves non-market forms of organisation.

Most people in the private sector work in large firms which are themselves bureaucracies, and the larger they are the more bureaucratic they tend to be. It has also been argued that we can think of firms as markets, with each employee having concluded a mutually agreeable contract with the firm, but in practice most employees occupy very standard jobs, are arranged in hierarchies, and follow rules.

We have already noted, too, that market exchange relies on some non-market elements. Buyer and seller need to have some shared understanding of what each is offering the other; they tend to look to government for a definition of the rules of exchange and the provision of a legal system to enforce them. Market transactions are governed by shared perceptions of fairness and appropriate behaviour, which may in turn become the basis of legal rules, e.g. governing door-to-door selling, or telemarketing.

At the large-scale level, too, there are questions about fairness – whether or not the logic of the market is sufficient justification for all corporate behaviour. Some writers on management have argued that we need to understand the firm in terms of its relationships with other groups – its shareholders, of course, but also its workers, its customers, its suppliers, the local community and various levels of government – who can be termed its 'stakeholders', and to whom it has obligations.

And while the market model implies instability – prices move up and down, firms enter the market and leave it, customers may buy one product today and a different one (or none at all) tomorrow – it is clear that much of business activity is concerned with minimising this instability and the uncertainty that goes with it. Firms may seek to stabilise their environment through takeovers or alliances. Consumer groups may demand a clear definition of the rights of the buyer. Industry associations may promulgate codes of practice, and call upon government to regulate the industry and exclude those who do not conform to standard practice. In other words, the conduct of 'business' may draw on shared norms and values, which are expressed as rules and enforced through the authority of government.

And at the small-scale level the market relationship may be quite unacceptable. One organisational researcher, Harold Garfinkel, sent students into department stores to haggle over the price of clearly marked items, e.g. offering \$4.50 for a shirt marked at \$5.95. The students found that not only were the store staff unwilling to bargain, they were often confused and anxious at being put into this situation. You might bargain over the price of a used car but not over a new shirt. The market relationship was not enough. Market relationships are important in business but so are other, non-market factors like trust and rules, as can be seen from the reaction to the relatively unfettered capitalism of the 1980s. Entrepreneurs were widely criticised for caring only about the market dimension. So 'market relations' cannot be equated with 'the private sector'.

The 'Third' Sector

Some observers now add to the traditional division between a public and a private sector a 'third sector'. This consists of organisations which are neither governmental nor profit seeking, but are brought together on the basis of affiliation: people seeing themselves as having something in common, and joining together on that basis. What they have in common could be ethnic origin, or religious belief, or an interest in a particular sport, or a concern for an issue of public policy, or some combination of these. Examples might include churches, charitable organisations, residents' groups, sporting clubs, etc. One can see why this could be seen as a sector of activity structured on the basis of affiliation.

But while a sense of affiliation may have brought the members together, organising the activity calls for routine and specialisation of tasks: someone has to collect the money, someone has to write the letters, someone has to sign the registration form. This leads to differentiation between office-bearers and members, and in larger organisations to a differentiation between paid staff, office-bearers and members. The relationship between them is defined in formal documents – rules and constitutions – and a clear hierarchy emerges, with full-time staff (recruited on the basis of their technical expertise rather than their standing in the group) tending to dominate the running of the organisation – a process which one early student of organisation (Michels) called 'the iron law of oligarchy'.

And while these organisations do not seek to make profits, they are, in a sense, in market competition with one another – for members, for support, for the ear of government, and for money. Every community organisation is seeking to tap the same pool of moral sentiment, and time, energy and money devoted to famine relief abroad cannot be devoted to the relief of multiple sclerosis at home. Union leaders may feel that the existence of many small unions weakens their impact, and seek to amalgamate with other unions to obtain a larger 'market share'. Community organisations are not immune from either bureaucratic or market forces, nor is affiliation confined to the community sector: people are more ready to follow orders from, or to do deals with, people that they know and trust.

We have to remember, too, that 'third sector' groups are often specifically oriented to government. A consumer group may be drawn together on the basis of a shared self-awareness (and therefore be located in the 'third sector'), but its focus is on the relationship between consumers and sellers (private sector), and it spends much of its time negotiating over possible action by government bodies (public sector). Exactly the same point could be made about a trade association.

Often organisations from one 'sector' will rely on action from another. A government welfare organisation may subsidise voluntary bodies to run children's homes. In this case it is likely to be concerned that the voluntary body employs qualified staff, and that its accounts are properly kept (i.e. kept to the satisfaction of government inspectors). For these reasons the 'non-government' body starts to look more and more like the government bodies to which it relates: it becomes an extension of the public 'sector'.

Linkage between Sectors

Talking about the world in terms of 'sectors' is so widely shared that it seems 'common sense'. There is a clear line drawn between the public sector and the private sector: they are different sorts of organisation, they have different concerns and they work in different ways.

But this clear separation does not seem to be confirmed by the experience of organisational participants or the evidence of researchers. They report that people from different sectors work closely together, and may even have their closest links with people outside their 'sector'. Farmers and their representatives, cooperatives, milk companies and government officials work closely together to organise the production and marketing of milk. The organisations through which this is done cannot be unambiguously allocated either to the private sector or to the public sector. Similarly, the need to provide for the care of the aged may give rise to close links between government officials, local authorities, families and community groups. Some officials have the specific job of creating a framework to bring together what is provided by government and what is provided by various forms of community activity. Again, what we end up with cannot be clearly allocated to one or other of the three 'sectors'.

So the observations do not fit our model of the world. There are several ways in which the student of organisation might respond. One is to see the observations as a form of deviant behaviour: there should be a clear separation between the concerns and operations of the public sector and those of the private. The fact that this distinction cannot be sustained in practice may be seen as messy but unobjectionable (often expressed in statements which begin 'in theory ...'). Or it may be seen as pathological, e.g. the government (public sector) has 'intervened' in the market (private sector) or, alternatively, the relevant part of the public sector has been 'captured' by the private sector 'vested interests' which it is supposed to control.

Alternatively, we could search for a new model in which the linkage between the sectors is less puzzling: the literature on 'corporatism' (sometime 'neo-corporatism') has emerged as a number of writers have attempted to do this.

The literature on corporatism is extensive and encompasses many varieties, but its core is the observation that in a number of western industrial societies, unions, employer organisations and government have come together not only for consultation but also to form policy, particularly on wages and employment matters, and (in the case of the first two) to enforce it on their members. This seems so much at variance with the assumptions of the three-sector model that the analysts searched for a new term and, drawing a parallel with pre-war Italy, labelled this sort of fusion of organised interests with government as 'corporatism'.

Corporatist analysis has been found to be helpful in the analysis of a range of industries in a number of countries. Organised interests are recognised and incorporated into the structure of government, and so it could be argued that they become part of the 'public sector'. At the same time, the official forms of government seem to have been taken over by the concerns of the private sector. So it is argued that these structures of 'incorporation' have to be seen as a new organisational form: corporatism.

These organisational changes seem quite common in industry, and similar processes have been reported in other fields such as care for the disabled, where the representatives of the disabled also seem to have been 'incorporated' into the official family. Cawson (1986) argues, though, that economic interests are much more likely to operate through these 'corporatist' patterns of representation than non-economic interests.

Corporatist analysis has a 'macro' focus: it recognises the importance of links between organisations and draws the implications for the way in which interests are represented in society. At the other end of the scale researchers have looked at the 'micro' level and asked 'what is involved in organisational work? How do people get things done?'. The answers have complemented the corporatist analysis: they have pointed to the way in which people in organisations develop links across organisational boundaries (and across the boundaries between sectors) in order to be able to get the cooperation of other organisations when it is needed. These researchers find that the structure of a single organisation is not enough to accomplish that organisation's work. It is necessary to draw on other organisations, and to do this hierarchical authority will probably not be enough. The organisational participant is likely to appeal both to incentives and to shared norms. In other words, you have to make other players part of your game, and in turn you have to become part of their games.

Overlap and Ambiguity

The 'sector' approach divides the world of organisation into three neat
compartments, and the 'linkage' approach looks at the way that people
keep boring holes in the walls between the compartments. A third
approach sees the task of dividing up the world of organisation in this
way as being quite futile, for several reasons.

Organisations are Themselves Alloys

They can't be divided into 'market', 'bureaucratic' and 'community'
organisations, because there are likely to be elements of all of these in
any organisation. It will not be the same in all organisations – the Stock
Exchange will be quite different from Greenpeace, and an organisation
in the 1990s may operate quite differently from the way that organisation worked in the 1950s. The task is to identify the nature of the mix,
not to place the organisation into one box or another. Our models are
analytic constructs, not empirical descriptions. We don't have them so
that we can divide actual organisations into 'hierarchies', 'markets', and
'communities', but so that we can see how, in any empirical case,
people make use of the various constituent elements to create and
maintain organisation.

Organisations Overlap

The different sorts of organisation exist simultaneously and overlie one
another, and drawing boundaries between their areas of concern is always
likely to be a bit artificial. The welfare of clothing outworkers who work
in their own homes making up clothing for a factory involves a range
of governmental bodies – concerned with health, factories, women's
affairs, possibly town planning – as well as the factory owners and
perhaps an organisation representing them. It may well draw in trade
unions, religious or ethnic groups, and in a quite different way, it may
reflect family structure in the group from which the workers are drawn.
It is possible to argue that it 'only' concerns the workers themselves
and their employer, but obviously it is possible for other organisations
to become involved in the question.

There are Alternative Ways of Organising, and These May Overlap

In the example we have just used, the welfare of the workers may be pursued through the unions, or through the family structure, through ethnic or religious bodies, or through the involvement of state bodies of various kinds.

The logic of this approach is that we should keep an open mind about how different sorts of organisation fit into the scheme of things. We should not make assumptions on the basis of definitions, e.g. that decisions about employment are simply market exchanges, or that the representation of workers is done by trade unions, but should ask how, in each case, people put the show together.

Review

1. In the real world there are a number of linked and overlapping organisations, rather than just 'The Organisation'.
2. People often talk about three 'sectors' of organisation: the public sector (or 'government'); the private sector (or 'business'); and a third sector (of non-profit or voluntary organisations, such as charities).
3. While bureaucratic forms of organisation may be dominant within the public sector it also includes autonomous agencies and professionals, horizontal as well as vertical links, and the use of norms and incentives to get its way.
4. Similarly, while market forms of organisation may predominate in the private sector it also includes bureaucratic organisation, notions of fairness, and codes of rules.
5. While common values may bring third-sector organisations into existence they often develop bureaucratic structures and compete with each other in a market-like way.
6. Links between parts of different sectors (e.g. government officials and their clients) may be as strong, or stronger than, links within each sector (e.g. between government departments).
7. Theories of 'corporatism' seek to explain these linkages between sectors in advanced industrial countries.
8. In any case, any organisation, large or small, is an alloy of organisational forms, each given a different weighting according to the circumstances.

Questions for Discussion

1. What 'market' and 'community' elements do you notice in the organisation of a 'public sector' organisation like the Post Office?
2. What organisational differences do you notice between publicly and privately owned universities?
3. Can you identify 'ambiguous' organisations that fit into more than one sector? What model of organisation predominates within them?
4. Look at a phone book: does it try to separate public from private sector? Why does it do so? Does it do so successfully? What other categorisations could you suggest?

Further Reading

Researchers have come up with many labels for the intermeshing of sectors. Some term these 'implementation structures' (Hjern and Porter (1981)). Others talk about 'issue networks' (Heclo (1978)) or 'governance regimes' (Campbell et al, eds (1991)). One of the most widely used terms has been 'policy community', which recognises the way that a shared interest in a particular policy field draws people from a variety of organisations into an organised relationship with one another, see Atkinson and Coleman (1992).

9 Organisation, Choice and Power

We have been studying organisation as a process, and something that people do. This is helpful in making sense of particular cases, but it does raise questions about the nature of organisation:

- does this imply choice, i.e. that people create the sort of organisations that they want, or need?
- does this leave power out of the picture?

In this chapter we will examine these questions, and ask what our approach suggests about the nature of organisation.

Organisation and Choice

Our analysis of organisation leads to a puzzle. On the one hand we have been analysing organisation as much as a process – as something that people do – as a thing. This seems to imply choice: that people end up with the organisation they have made for themselves. On the other hand the overwhelming image that we have of organisation is of a powerful constraint on our freedom of action. In popular usage, 'the organisation' or 'the system' or just 'they' is a potent and probably unbeatable force. Max Weber, the pioneer theorist of bureaucracy, labelled it 'the iron cage'. How can people be so constrained by something they themselves have created?

We have seen that organisation links people in ways that enable their individual efforts to accomplish collectively things they could not do individually (and which they may not have any particular interest in bringing about). In this sense, organisation is a positive force: it expands people's capacity for action.

At the same time, it can only do this by restricting their vision of what the organisation is doing, and their ability to exercise their own judgement and make their own choices about what is to come out of the organisational activity in which they are engaged. Phrases like 'don't ask me. I only work here' have become clichés because they express a shared perception of organisation as something which detracts from the ordinary capacity of human beings. In this sense, organisation is a negative force: it contracts people's capacity for action.

There is no real contradiction here: organisation expands the capacity of collectivities by contracting the autonomy of individuals. It enables concerted action but it restrains individuals' capacity to act. This means that people are likely to feel ambiguous about organisation: they often feel a reluctance to take responsibility for something that is outside their control, which is the feeling expressed in such phrases as 'I only work here'. When discussed in this way organisation becomes something outside of us, the working of an outside force of which we have imperfect knowledge and over which we have little control: 'They'.

This reflects the fact that organisation is about inertia – that is, about continuing in the direction that we've been going. Organisation stabilises action. It makes predictable the actions of the participants: we have a reasonable idea of what the counter clerk in the social security office will or won't do. In a sense, the action has an existence of its own: it's there, waiting for people to put it into action; it has become *institutionalised*.

Going back to our football example, we can see that the role of umpire has become institutionalised: you can decide whether to have an umpire or not, but you're not likely to sit around discussing what the umpire should do.

So what people can do in organisations is channelled and limited in a number of ways. People who join organisations realise this. As one local government councillor put it, 'Joining the council is like coming in to Act III of a play.' Your scope for action is very much limited by what's gone before. But this raises questions about relationships in the organisation: to continue the metaphor, does this mean that the people who were there in Act I and Act II have the advantage over their colleagues? This question directs our attention back to the origins of organisations, and to the way in which ideas about origins are used in practice. With time, the origins of organisations become obscure, but they become a source of validating myths: that is, references to origins are used to justify and explain things that are done and the standing of particular participants in the organisation.

But if what people can do in organisations is shaped by the past, do they really have any choice? This is one of the fundamental puzzles in social analysis: the relationship between structure and action. We have spoken of organisation as a pattern of action. But at the same time there seems to be something there that is more than action, something more independent of the actors: something called 'structure'. If they are both part of the picture, which comes first: does the action produce the structure, or does the structure produce the action?

The simple answer to this complex question seems to be 'both': the structure tells people how to act, and when they act in that way, they reinforce and recreate the structure. For instance, as a general rule, schools are organisations which are hierarchical in structure. The teacher who walks into a classroom and calls for quiet so that the lesson can begin is relying on this hierarchical structure, under which students defer to teachers (in these circumstances). When the students recognise this and fall silent their action recognises the hierarchical structure, reinforces it, and strengthens the likelihood that teachers and students will behave like this in the future. In this way structure informs action and action reproduces the structure – which leads Anthony Giddens to argue that we have to think of structure as being necessarily tied to action, and that it therefore is more helpful to think not of the structure of organisation but of the circular process by which this structure is produced and reproduced, a process he terms 'structuration'.

We see here the elements of choice and constraint: the students who fell silent at the teacher's request did have the option of ignoring it, and in that sense they chose to accept the demands of a hierarchical structure. But this was not a totally free-floating choice: it was part of a flow of situations where teachers gave the cues and students followed them. There were other situations, e.g. in the playground, where it would be inappropriate for a teacher to demand silence, but in the classroom it was appropriate.

So to keep talking when everyone else had fallen silent would be to stand outside this known pattern of behaviour. Many students might not even be conscious of making a choice: that was just how it was at school, they might say. And yet they would recognise that the deference would be greater in some schools, or with some years, or with some teachers, than with others. In other words, the structure did not totally determine the action: it indicated an appropriate course of action, but how closely people followed this was a choice for them. So there was both pattern and choice – or structure and action.

In this context we can see formal organisation as a continuing flow of patterned action. One particularly powerful source of pattern is occupational differentiation. Specialised occupations are bodies of people who have been trained to see the world in a particular way and to act in a particular way. The engineer sees the road-building programme as an opportunity for the exercise of engineering skills; the accountant sees it as an area in need of cost control. We can talk about this as a 'choice' that each has made, but it would be more realistic to see it as a structured response – structured by the skills and orientations and routines of the profession in question, and the individual's place in the organisation.

Organisation and Power

To speak of organisation as something that people make also raises questions about power. The most casual observer of organisation would conclude that even though organisation is the product of action by those involved, not all outcomes are equally possible, nor are all people equally significant, and that the differences are a continuing part of the organisational process. To recognise these differences is to recognise power as a dimension of organisation. In a rationalist, mechanical model of organisation, questions of power are out of place. That there are power relationships in organisation remains one of those dimensions of organisation that everyone knows about and people talk about but which does not appear in the writing: it is too 'profane'. Once we have recognised the existence of power we have to confront questions about power relationships *within* an organisation, *between* an organisation and the outsiders who deal with it, and *among* organisations.

Power within Organisations

To describe an organisation as a pattern of power relations seems to be consistent with the experience that most people have of organisation. One of the most common ways to depict an organisation is as a triangle, with a few people at the top giving directions to a much larger group of workers at the bottom. This is the 'common-sense' view of organisation, but the student (working from this book) would note that it is based on the bureaucratic model, and sees organisation as a pattern of authorised directions. That is, 'power' in organisation is not brute force or coercion but accepted inequality or legitimate authority.

In this perspective an organisation is a triangular hierarchy of authority, with the people at the top having the most and the people at the bottom the least. To the extent that 'power' is seen as the capacity to give authorised directions, it is therefore an integral part of organisation, but not a problem. But as we have seen from our discussion of 'bureaucratic failure' this is often not the case: the people at the apex of the triangle may have considerable difficulty in making their authority carry all the way down the line. So it may be quite misleading to assume that the distribution of power in the organisation can be determined from the organisation chart.

The question of power becomes more complex when we take into account the market perspective. Using that perspective, we can see organisation in terms of self-interested exchanges between individuals. Power would be seen as the capacity to strike these deals, i.e. market power. So the people at the apex of the triangle are seen as contracting with all the workers at different levels to secure their services in exchange for an agreed income and other benefits, and the organisation is seen as a pattern of self-interested exchanges. This is not to argue that an organisation would fall wholly into the 'market' pattern. Those who write from this perspective, like Williamson and Ouchi, argue that some sorts of work are best accomplished through bureaucratic relationships, some best done through a market framework, and an organisation will choose the most efficient form in each case.

In this market perspective the distribution of power usually matches the distribution of authority. The people who have authority also have the money, and the more significant you are in the organisational hierarchy, the more reward you can demand. But there are likely to be some deviations when workers can demand a level of reward quite disproportionate to their hierarchical rank, e.g. when they possess skills which are hard to replace.

But these deviations are easily explained within the market model: these people simply have a price on the labour market which does not reflect their importance in the organisational hierarchy. However, Ouchi argues that self-interested contracting cannot always be relied on, because sometimes it is not possible to specify in detail what constitutes a good job. For instance, it is difficult to specify in advance exactly what a surgeon should do. In these cases, it is argued that neither hierarchy nor market provides an adequate organisational base, and a 'horizontal' form of organisation (which Ouchi calls the 'clan') needs to be invoked. In the case of the surgeon, the employer, whether it is the hospital or the patient or the insurance company, tends to rely on validation by the profession itself: other surgeons say what a good surgeon should do, and the profession of surgery becomes a significant organisational form.

Moreover, there seem to be positions of power in organisations which can't be related to any real or notional contracting with the people at the apex. In a classical piece of organisational research, Michel Crozier found that the maintenance engineers in a tobacco factory were powerful in that they possessed a high degree of autonomy: nobody pushed them around. This was because their skills were essential and difficult to replace: if the machines broke down production stopped, and so the people who could repair the machines were highly valued. So they had a position of power in the organisation which was quite independent of the wishes of those at the top of the hierarchy, and reflected more the nature of the work process.

So while there is some reason to see power as part of the development of market transactions within organisations there seem to be a number of loose ends. People can have market power which far exceeds their bureaucratic authority, or they can have bureaucratic authority which is not reflected in their market power. The market framework does not so much explain the distribution of power within the organisation; rather, it introduces a further source of complexity.

We started with a presentation of power in organisation as something that flows from the structure of authority; this was challenged and limited by the application of the market perspective. It is also challenged by the application of the community perspective which sees the organisation as a group of people cohering around shared norms. How does this sort of cohesion affect power relations?

In one sense it can be regarded as reinforcing hierarchical authority. The people at the apex of the triangle give directions, but they also assert values for the organisation, through speeches and reports and newsletters and other elements of the organisational process. The ability of the hierarchy to proclaim the dominant values for the organisation can be seen as an additional source of power.

But on the other hand the cohesion and the values may not be those of the hierarchy. The work-group is itself an organisational identity, and may be more important in shaping what people do than the organisation itself. Studies have suggested that soldiers in wartime give their first loyalty to the immediate unit – the face-to-face group of 'buddies' whom they know – rather than to the army or to their country. And during the failed Moscow coup of August 1991, when the special KGB commando squad was ordered to attack the Russian parliament building, 'the rank and file polled one another and unanimously decided to disobey'.

There is a structural tension here: the hierarchy relies on these community norms to produce the cohesion and loyalty that the army needs, but at the same time these shared norms are a potential challenge to hierarchical control. People at the bottom of the organisation may be more interested in what their fellow workers think of them than in what the people at the top say about the organisation. And this can go right up the line. For instance, in January 1993 the newly elected President Clinton sought to remove the ban on homosexuals in the US armed forces, but met with vigorous opposition from the armed forces chiefs. They were his sworn subordinates but they were more responsive to the norms of the armed forces than to their duty to obey the president.

The community norms which are a potential challenge to hierarchical authority may also be located outside the organisation. The professions, for instance, are always a potential problem for organisations. The professionals bring their knowledge to the organisation but they also bring a 'horizontal' allegiance to their fellow professionals, and can assert this against the demands of the organisational hierarchy.

And there are the other identities that people have outside the organisation which have nothing to do with its work but which may be a source of community solidarity which can cut across the wishes of the organisational hierarchy. Religious beliefs, for instance, may have a bearing on the willingness of health workers to comply with central directives on abortion. Ethnic or regional origin, place of residence, or school attendance can all be sources of community solidarity within organisations, and as such a challenge to hierarchical authority.

Power Between Organisations and Outsiders

We have tried to keep this discussion of power relatively simple by limiting ourselves to power *within* organisations: what about power relations *between* organisations and the people outside them? This is where much of the 'common-sense' knowledge about organisation and power is generated. When we experience organisations as outsiders – across a desk, or at the end of a telephone – we often feel powerless against their inflexibility.

Here again, the bureaucratic model seems to orient the discussion. Counter staff are seen to be responding to the organisation rather than the client because bosses give them orders while clients cannot. But this assumes that the client has nowhere else to go or that the organisation doesn't mind whether the client stays around or not. In other words, if we mobilised the market framework would the existence of market choice make a difference to this impression of organisational dominance? In a famous study called *Exit, Voice and Loyalty* (1970) Hirschman argued that it did. Where the service was a monopoly and customers were unable to leave, the organisation had no incentive to be responsive to them. Where customers were free to leave they could express their discontent ('voice') or take their custom elsewhere ('exit'), and the evidence suggested that this left customers in a more powerful position.

Alternatively, if we bring the community model into the discussion, the power of the organisation over the outsiders is vulnerable to the links that can grow up between officials and their clients. The officials may take on the perspective of the locals, rather than that of the centre – a process known as 'going native'. Again, the centre wants to have good local links; what goes with this is the possible erosion of central control.

Power between Organisations

We should now turn briefly to the question of power *between* organisations, because much of the action in organisations concerns dealing with other organisations. In these circumstances, the authority model is likely to be much less significant. If you have to deal with someone in another organisation it is unlikely that you will be able to appeal to some boss who can issue an authorised direction. We need to look at the other models as well. The market model raises questions of interest and exchange, and impels us to ask 'to what extent can these organisations offer benefits to one another? Or inflict damage? Does the nature of this balance make them more or less likely to defer to the other?' In other words, are they likely to have a power relationship which flows from interested exchange?

On the other side of the page the community model has also proved helpful in understanding the power relations among organisations. Research has suggested that when organisations cannot coerce one another, particularly when they have to deal with one another over a long period of time, the officials involved will tend to develop what might be called 'trading relations'. They will acquire an understanding of the main concerns of the other parties, and a respect for their positions, realising that these have to be taken seriously in any deals. They are likely to place a lot of stress on 'trust', which may mean not only personal integrity but also the ability to get things done. That is, they try to develop the ability to deal with one another on a continuing basis, and in this context 'power' is a function of how effectively you can take part in this sort of trading: someone who knows what they want and has a reputation for being backed up by their own organisation will carry more weight in the game than someone who is indecisive and unsure about whether they can count on support from their home base.

Power in General

We started our discussion of the question of power in organisation in terms of interpersonal relations within a single organisation, but we have been led beyond this, in several ways. In the first place, we have had to take notice of the multi-organisational dimension: to understand the power relations in an organisation you need to be able to look outside it. Secondly, the concept of 'power' seems to convey different things in our different models, and different sorts of power may be in operation at the one time, and these may cut across one another. These factors make power relationships more ambiguous and contestable than the straight hierarchical model suggests.

This leads us to a central theoretical argument in the social sciences about the nature of power, which we cannot explore in detail, but whose application to organisation we need to note.

In the right corner there is the classic Weberian approach: power is defined as the likelihood that someone will get their way despite resistance from others. The political scientist Robert Dahl defined power in terms of influence, in particular that 'A influences B to the extent that A gets B to do something that B would not otherwise do' (1963: 41). In this perspective, power is something that is seen in what people do, usually to other people, and can be observed in specific episodes. Dahl's study of power in an American city, *Who Governs?* (1961) approached the question by taking a number of contested issues, finding out who the leading players were, and who won and who lost. This approach would clearly be easily applicable to organisations.

In the left corner are those who argue, first, that defining power in terms of winning battles can be slightly misleading, since not having to fight battles may be even clearer evidence of power. They go on to argue that the exercise of power should be seen in the routine practice and the taken-for-granted of everyday life, rather than in the occasional set-piece battles. To understand power in organisation, they say, we have to ask questions about what people do routinely, how questions are defined, and what is seen as good and appropriate practice. In this perspective, power in organisations is much more diffuse and structural, as much a consequence of the way the game is played as it is an attribute of the players. It is something to be seen in the micropolitics of daily practice as much as in the drama of formal decisions.

In some ways, this is a dispute about what it is that we focus our attention on when we are studying organisation. The first approach concentrates on the set-piece battles of organisational life: identifiable decision points around which the opposed sides have gathered. The second approach has its focus on the patterning of organisational life which produces this outcome – the arenas in which the contest is conducted, the understandings the contestants share, the commitments that have been established, etc. So, confronted with the same statement about power in organisation (e.g. 'the Treasury always wins'), the first perspective would look for evidence of the success of Treasury in open contests, while the second would look for the pattern of beliefs and practices which underlies both the open contests, and the more prevalent structured but uncontested application of the same perspective.

This calls for a more subtle conceptualisation of power. An influential approach is that of Stephen Lukes (1974), who argues for a three-dimensional model of power:

- the first dimension is to do with formal decisions
- the second is to do with the way in which the action is channelled to make some outcomes more likely than others
- the third has to do with the shared understandings and knowledge which frame both the question and the way it is answered.

The first dimension of power is most evident in the bureaucratic model of organisation. People give and take orders, and justify their activity by referring to decisions reached beforehand. In the market model, wage bargaining and employment contracts are examples of transactions in which power is visible and contested. The employer has other people available to hire, but the employee has to work to live. However, the visible, contested exercise of power is more often taken as evidence of 'market failure', such as the existence of monopolies which can put the squeeze on their suppliers or consumers. Visible contests in which one side wins and one side loses are also evident in the community model, particularly when people come to mobilise their friends or kinfolk in 'self-help retaliation' for wrongs done to them.

The second dimension of power is expressed in the rules and regulations that determine what gets on the agenda for decision in a bureaucratic organisation. In the market model, the second dimension may be expressed in several ways: barriers to entry that prevent people getting on to the playing field; pre-existing or inherited inequalities of income that make the players unequal before they start; and externalities, in which people are not included in making deals that nevertheless will affect them. The second dimension is also present in community forms of organisation in which gossip and supernatural sanctions may ensure that issues discomforting to the powerful are not raised. Scott (1990) points out there is often a half-hidden, unofficial discourse of the powerless, expressed in jokes and proverbs that criticise the powerful while falling short of provoking retaliation). To the extent that people really believe the self-justifications of the powerful then we can say Lukes's third dimension of power is operating.

The shared understandings of Lukes's 'third dimension' are not the property of any particular model. Rather, each model is itself a set of shared understandings about how to act in particular cicumstances: following rules; self-interestedly; or by reference to the norms and values of a group. The 'third-dimensional' question then becomes: how do some people's definition of the situation triumph over others'? How for example have we come to regard the 'market' model as predominant in the production and exchange of goods? Why do we regard the 'bureaucratic' model as predominant in government? Why do we see 'the family' as a form of community? Who constitutes the 'we' in these questions, and who is excluded?

Review

1. Organisation seems both to limit and expand individuals' capacity for action.
2. The more 'institutionalised' organisations become, the more they seem to exist independently of particular individual actions.
3. People more often join established organisations rather than invent new ones.
4. Stories about the origins of organisations are used to validate current activity.

5. The relationship between structure and action is reciprocal and repetitive: action reproduces structure; structure constrains action.
6. The bureaucratic model sees power flowing down an organisational hierachy.
7. The market model also allows for unequal distribution of rewards, depending in part on a person's strategic position in the process of work.
8. Common norms and values, however, may subvert as well as sustain organisational hierarchies.
9. Power over clients and customers depends in part on whether they have alternatives to go to.
10. Market and community models are more effective than hierarchy at explaining relations between organisations.
11. Power can be conceptualised on the one hand as involving visible decisions within organisations, and on the other hand as the effect of less visible patterns of organisation that allow some issues to emerge for decision while suppressing others.

Questions for Discussion

1. Rank a group of organisations you are familiar with according to their degree of institutionalisation.
2. In what ways is the structure of the university reproduced by the action of its members (and in what ways is it undermined)?
3. What is the different balance of choice and constraint in the following pairs of organisation?

    • school and family
    • school and university/college
    • university/college and paid employment
    • university/college and being on social security
    • social security and paid employment.

4. In what ways is the downward flow of power through the school or university/college hierarchy frustrated?
5. In what ways does the pattern of hierarchical positions in the school or university/college diverge from the pattern of financial rewards, and why is there a divergence?

6. To what extent do the norms and values of the school or university/college reinforce the power of senior members, and to what extent do they limit or subvert it?
7. To what extent does the school's or university's/college's power over students depend on students' lack of alternatives?
8. Give examples of (a) the episodic use of power against resistance and (b) more diffuse, structural use of power in (i) a lecture, (ii) the classroom or a tutorial and (iii) a family.

Further Reading

Mintzberg (1983) is a comprehensive and empirically grounded discussion of power in organisations, while Clegg (1989) offers a more analytical and theoretical treatment of the question. Giddens's argument about action and structure can be found in Chapter 1 of his *The Constitution of Society* (1984). The argument about transaction costs as an explanation of organisational structure was made by Williamson (1975) and developed by Ouchi (1980). Crozier (1963) studied power relationships in several workplaces, and Hirschman (1970) explored the power relationships between organisations and their clients. Dahl (1961) is a study of power in a community; the definition quoted comes from Dahl (1963). Lukes (1974) is a particularly useful discussion of different types of power. On the avoidance of the 'profane' in discussions of organisation, see Colebatch and Degeling (1986). On the development of trading relationships between organisations, see Mintzberg (1983).

10 Evaluating Organisation

Evaluating organisation, like speaking prose, is something we do all the time, usually without realising it. 'Isn't that typical of the Taxation Office?' or 'Student Administration never ask you to fill in one form when two will do' are examples of the 'common-sense' evaluations of organisation which we hear every day. But what sort of evaluation of organisational action would follow from the analysis of organisation developed here?

There is a 'common-sense' perspective in which the evaluation of organisation is relatively straightforward. An organisation is an instrument for the accomplishment of authorised purposes. It can be evaluated by ascertaining to what extent it achieved these objectives (effectiveness), and what level of resources it needed to do so (efficiency).

This sort of evaluation requires a clear statement of the objectives of the organisation. As long as they are clear, consistent with one another, and readily measurable, evaluating the extent to which the organisation has achieved them is relatively straightforward. The question is how likely it is that these conditions will be met, and what happens to evaluation when they are not.

While a clear perception of organisational objectives is an important element in this instrumental model of organisation, in practice many organisations cannot point to a clear statement of objectives. There may be no statement of objectives at all, or they may be stated in such vague terms as to provide little help in the evaluation of the organisation's performance, e.g. a statement that 'the objective of this organisation is excellence' would not be much use in evaluating the organisation's performance (though it could be significant: one would need to discover what use was made of it in the work of that organisation).

It may be that objectives are stated but that they are not consistent with one another. A manufacturing company may declare its objectives to be (a) to increase profits, (b) to increase market share, and (c) to be at the forefront of technological development. These objectives 'hang together', but they may cut across one another. Increasing expenditure on research and development may keep the company technologically advanced, but it would have to be financed from earnings. A vigorous marketing push into new territory, with a lot of promotion and discounting, may increase market share but at the expense (in the short term, at least) of earnings. So, while the statement of objectives may be useful in the evaluation, in order for it to be operational there would need to be further work – either by the organisation or by the evaluator – on how the different objectives were to be traded off against one another.

Finally, the analyst may decide that the organisation has other objectives which are unlikely to be stated openly. The programme of grants to local sporting clubs may have 'promotion of amateur sport' as its stated objective, but 'securing the re-election of the local MP' might be another objective. Similarly, a family-owned company may be running a transport operation which is at best marginally profitable, and justify this by saying 'our grandfather started out in transport, and we want to retain a presence in that industry', i.e. family sentiment would have to be regarded as an objective. Or a media company which makes its money from sensational tabloid journalism may buy a loss-making 'serious' newspaper in order to lend respectability to the group as a whole.

Again, the absence of clearly stated objectives makes it difficult to do the straightforward 'balance sheet' exercise, but in this case it would be pointless asking the participants to make a clear statement of their objectives.

Even if these problems could be overcome, and we could derive a clear statement of objectives for any given organisation, we would be doing this on the assumption that the organisation should be evaluated in terms of its own objectives. In reality people are likely to evaluate an organisation on their own terms as well as on the organisation's terms. Treasury officials (governmental or corporate) may evaluate it in terms of whether or not it will make a financial demand on the treasury. Clients may evaluate it in terms of how responsive it is to their needs. The women's movement may evaluate it in terms of how many women have reached the senior ranks of the organisation.

So evaluation is unlikely to resemble the simple balance sheet with which we started out, and in fact part of the work of evaluating organisational activity is clarifying the terms in which it is to be done. In trying to clarify these terms it is useful to turn again to the three organisational models: market, hierarchy and community. What approach to evaluation would be taken in each of these models?

In the market model the organisation is seen as an exchange based on the mutual self-interest of the organisation and its clients. The evaluator would be asking if both sides were satisfied with the deal. On the one hand, is there a demand for the organisation's product, and on the other, is the organisation meeting the demands of its clientele?

In the authority model the organisation is seen as an instrument for the accomplishment of approved goals, and the question would be what these goals were, and whether or not they were achieved. This is as the 'common-sense' model with which we started.

In the community model the organisation is seen as the expression of the community's interest in a particular area of concern, and the question for the evaluator might be 'does the organisation, in its activities and its accomplishments, reflect the community and its values?'

In applying these approaches to the evaluation of organisation, we find that they tend to raise other questions, and often overflow into the other approaches. The market approach, for instance, sees organisation as an exchange between two parties – but who are the two parties? Customers, presumably, and the organisation – but does that mean those who work in it, or those who own it? And should anyone else be involved? Consider this hypothetical case:

> *The Able Manufacturing Company has for many years been manufacturing specialised mining equipment. It has always returned a decent profit, and has a good number of loyal customers, many of them overseas. It was recently bought by a conglomerate which has no interest in manufacturing, but considered that the factory site would be an ideal location for the tourist hotel and office complex which it has been planning. It therefore decides to shut down the factory, sack the workers and wind up the company.*

The owners of the company had evaluated its operations and decided to close it down. But this case raises the question of whose opinion should be taken into account in the evaluation. The owners may have done better as a result of closing down the factory, but many other people associated with the factory had lost out. These included the workers who were sacked, the suppliers, the customers, the local business community, and even the government's export promotion agency. This is why some management writers have started to talk of companies as being made up of a network of 'stakeholders' – not just those who own shares, but those who have a stake in its activities: workers, managers, bankers, shareholders, suppliers, customers, and relevant others. So even when the question is cast in the 'market' mode we find ourselves slipping into a consideration of some sort of community of interest, out there in the market.

The argument that market choice provides a way of evaluating organisational activity rests on the assumption that there are (or could be) a number of alternative suppliers, and that there is a price attached to the service being supplied. What if these conditions do not apply? If the gas company supplies a stable and steadily increasing number of customers, but is the only gas supplier in town, can any evaluative conclusions be drawn? Or consider the relationship between a department of agriculture and the farmers' unions. They are certainly the customers of the department, and probably give it strong support, but then they do not have to pay for its services. If they had to pay the full cost of the department's services they might decide that they could buy these services more cheaply from Consolidated Agribusiness International. Does this mean that evaluating through the market requires a price system and competitive suppliers? And if so, is it much use in government, where these conditions are usually absent ?

We have already explored some of the problems involved in the evaluation of organisations as instruments for the accomplishment of authorised objectives. It was not always easy to define what those objectives might be. And this assumed that we had the right question, i.e. that the problem was to define the objectives.

Let us go back to the original assumption of instrumentality. Supposing that the founders of the organisation had objectives, that they recruited experts for this purpose, and placed them in organisations which were dedicated to these specialised skills: the Survey Office, for instance, or the Water Supply Department. In this organisational structure there is an in-built force to acquire and manifest expertise in these named fields: the Survey Office will want to do more and better surveys, and the Water Supply Department will want to build more and better water supplies. These could be counted as additional objectives which have been smuggled in along the way. They are not so much ends as processes in which the experts wish to be engaged: 'getting there is half the fun'. This suggests that an evaluation of an organisation solely in terms of objectives is likely to be incomplete.

Turning now to the use of the 'community' framework for the evaluation of organisation, one of the first questions we encounter is 'which community are we talking about?' Is it the community at large, or some smaller and more specific community? We have already noted the close and mutually supportive relationship between a department of agriculture and its constituents. A smoothly operating relationship of this sort could be evaluated as successful organisation, or it could be evaluated as the reverse: as the 'capture' of the organisation by a particular interest, at the expense of the community as a whole.

Here, we have to remember that organisations (particularly in government) tend to be specialised, and to be closely linked to other bodies sharing that specialised interest – professional groups, industry associations, unions, etc. Organised interests seek to get their concerns inscribed on state agendas by the establishment: conservationists want a conservation agency, timber companies want a forestry agency, women's groups want a women's agency, etc. So it might be expected that there will be a 'community' linked to each agency. Would the evaluator want to know how well the activities of the agency reflected the values of this particular community, or would it be the values of the wider community (which might have less interest in these concerns)? Should the women's agency be evaluated in terms of the values of the women's lobby or those of the community as a whole?

Even if we could reach broad agreement on the values to be pursued there would still be questions about the way in which these were to be applied. For instance, agreement on equal employment opportunity as a value would still leave questions about whether what was being valued was equality (the same treatment for all) or equity (fair treatment for all, which may mean special treatment for some). Again, is the value to be understood in procedural terms (men and women compete for appointment on the same terms) or in substantive terms (the appointee is as likely to be female as male)?

The discussion so far has rested on the assumption that the evaluation of organisation means just that. However, in almost every field in which many organisations operate they may have different understandings of the task, and there may be a range of legal/constitutional arrangements relating them to one another. Consequently, the participants in these complex organisational fields have to learn to develop ways of dealing with one another which recognise the distinct interests of the different participants. At the same time there is ample scope for reformers to 'discover' that there is a great deal of confusion and overlap in the field, and a 'need' for a clear and rational demarcation of responsibility.

It is clear from the discussion so far that different people can evaluate the same piece of organisational activity in different ways. In part, this reflects the fact that they are likely to approach the task with different analytical perspectives, and this is related to their differing positions in the action.

Let us take the example of taxi driving. Often, taxi drivers do not own the taxis they drive but pay the owner a fixed amount for the use of the taxi for a certain time. It is then up to them to make enough in fares to cover the cost of the hire and the fuel; what remains is their income for that day's work. Often, the taxi driver will make less from twelve hours' work than an ordinary labourer makes in eight hours: how would we evaluate this way of organising taxi transport?

The evaluation would reflect both position in the game and analytic approach. An academic economist of the free-market persuasion would say that this was both efficient and fair: if taxi drivers were not satisfied with the money they earned, they would stop taxi driving and turn to some other form of employment. Either they would be replaced by other drivers who were prepared to work for that level of income, or they would not, in which case taxis would be a bit harder to find, and this might push the hire rates up, and so attract drivers back into the industry.

The taxi user would probably agree with the economist's analysis, but complain that when you most needed a taxi you could never find one because everyone wanted one at the same time.

For an official of the transport workers' union, though, the low income of taxi drivers might be seen as evidence of a need for government action, e.g. making a rule to fix a minimum rate of pay. This union official would see the drivers' acceptance of low earnings not as an example of efficient market exchange but as evidence of exploitation.

Finally, for a feature writer on a Sunday paper, this form of organisation could provide the basis for a story on the hard life of a taxi driver, with photos of a typical driver and the family that he or she never has time to see. The story would be appealing to community values: the perception of a fair day's pay for a day's work.

Clearly, the evaluation of organisation is a game that anyone can play, but it is possible to play it with more or less skill. Playing with more skill requires a certain amount of introspection: being aware of both the analytic approach being employed, and the position in the action – or to put it another way, where you were coming from, and where you were at. In making this much clear the evaluator would also be clarifying the fact that other participants in the game might evaluate the same action in different ways.

The practical significance is that while it may be convenient to think of evaluation as a simple, one-off exercise, like an annual audit of the organisation's accounts, in practice it is more like the construction of a framework for discourse among people who are interested in the same thing, but for different reasons. The process of evaluation can be formalised in a variety of ways. It may be a matter of organisational routine, e.g. when a government department, giving a grant to a community group to run a service, requires a formal evaluation of the service every three years. Or the evaluation may come at a time of crisis, and take the form of a Royal Commission. In addition there is the evaluation of organisation which takes place outside the formal framework, e.g. by the press. In each case there is evaluation but it means something different: what it is depends on what people make of it.

Review

1. Organisations are typically evaluated according to their objectives, but in practice these are often vague, inconsistent, or hidden.
2. Organisations are often evaluated in terms of others' objectives, not their own.
3. The market model suggests evaluation in terms of mutual satisfaction of buyer and seller, but:

    • there may be other 'stakeholders'
    • the clients may have no choice to allow comparison.

4. The community model suggests evaluation in terms of meshing norms and values, but:

    • interaction with clients may have diverted the organisation from its original purposes
    • evaluators may not be truly representative of their communities.

5. Any particular activity can be evaluated from a number of different standpoints.
6. Evaluation is not a once-and-for-all operation but part of the routine activity of all organisations.

Questions for Discussion

1. What are the objectives of the school or university/college, and to what extent are they clear, consistent and undisguised?

2. How would we measure the achievement of these objectives?
3. To what extent is the school or university/college successful in reflecting community norms and values (and should it be)?
4. Who, apart from staff and students are 'stakeholders' in the school or university/college?
5. Identify groups of experts within the school or university/college whose goals may be smuggled into the wider purposes?
6. To what extent can students evaluate the school or university/college by comparison with alternatives?
7. In what circumstances may staff be captured by students, or student representatives fail to represent their community?
8. In what ways would evaluations of the school or university/college by the following differ from each other?

   * an academic economist
   * a union leader
   * a member of a women's group
   * the leader writer in a newspaper.

Further Reading

Pressman and Wildavsky's (1984) study of implementation shows how the different participants in joint action have different criteria for success. Legge (1984) and Uhr, ed (1991) discuss evaluation.

11 Conclusions

In this book we have developed a particular approach to understanding organisation. Where has it taken us, and where can we go from here?

Organisation and Organising

We focused on the activity of organising rather than on organisations. We have seen organisation as something that people do. Certainly, there are things called 'organisations', but they exist because people have called them into being, and they operate in the way that people make them work. In other words, an organisation is a pattern of action, and the questions for organisational analysis are what this pattern is, and how it got there. We could call this an 'action-centred' approach, one whose focus is on the process ('organising', as Weick puts it) rather than the outcome ('organisation').

When people constitute and maintain a pattern of action (i.e. when they organise), they draw on existing models – patterns which they and other people know from previous experience and which are seen as an appropriate basis for working together. We identified three such models:

- market: people organise through individual exchanges which serve their interests
- bureaucracy: people organise by following rules defined by hierarchic authority
- community: people organise by acting in ways which are appropriate for some group of which they are a part.

These models are not sorting boxes for empirical examples. It is not that some organisations are markets while others are hierarchies: all organisations will have some elements of each model, but what is the nature of the mix, and how does it vary within and between organisations?

For instance, when new employees join a firm there is always a lot that they don't know about how things are done. To what extent is it left to them to find their way around, on the basis that it's in their own interest to find out (i.e. market)? Does the firm direct someone to organise orientation activities and tell the new employees to attend (bureaucracy)? Do the existing employees take it on themselves to instruct the newcomers (community)? All of these are possible, and all of them may happen; what we need to understand is the nature of the mix.

Organisation as Rational Instruments

This way of thinking about organisation seems to cut across common sense. Much of the thinking and writing on organisation sees organisations as a rational response to problems: we have organisation because there is something to be done which could not be achieved by individuals acting alone. Organisation is the instrument people use to accomplish these goals. Alternative forms of organisation are possible: people may prefer some forms to others. Some forms may work better than others. People choose the form that works best for them.

The emphasis here is on the individual, and on individual choice: organisations are, in this perspective, the aggregations of individual decisions. Individuals are confronted by options, and in choosing among these options they express their preferences. This perspective on organisation tends to imagine an unorganised world, and ask how individuals might decide to form or join (or not to form or join) organisations. They deal with situations of choice, and they seem to be confronting it for the first time. The stories are sometimes called 'contractarian' because they lie in a tradition of political philosophy that explored the conditions in which people – typically men – in a state of nature might form a 'social contract' – that is, that forms of political organisation are best understood as the consequence of a bargain struck between otherwise free individuals. This directs our attention to the terms of the bargain, and the discussion assumes rational, utility-maximising individuals, i.e. people who will do what's best for them.

One of the difficulties with this approach is the assumption that people can make a rational choice about what's in their best interest: i.e. that they know what the alternative courses of action are and their consequences, and can weigh the options in terms of how well the outcomes match their interests, and choose accordingly. But as we have seen there are practical limits on the capacity of organisational participants to make this sort of rational choice ('bounded rationality'), and it has been argued that often the framework of rational choice is more of symbolic than substantitive importance.

In this context, while we may speak as though people have chosen a particular set of organisational arrangements, usually the organisation was there before the people. Organisations are continuing things: they are already running when we arrive on the scene, and we find ourselves confronted with an existing order. Occasionally, we may be part of the setting up of an organisation. We are likely to find that there are many things determining the nature of the organisational arrangements apart from the preferences of the founders, including the expectations of the people with whom the organisation deals, and the requirements of legal registration. So, while the attitudes of the people who use it are clearly relevant in shaping the organisational order, it is misleading to regard it simply as something that they have chosen.

The perception of organisations as the instruments that people choose to accomplish their ends also overlooks the extent to which organisations themselves shape the action. A housing corporation, for example, can be seen as the instrument the government has chosen to deal with the problem of youth homelessness, but it must also be recognised as a particular way of defining the question, and the answer. It is likely to define youth homelessness in terms of a 'housing shortfall', and advocate attacking it by building more units of housing. A family services agency, by contrast, might diagnose the problem as stemming from the breakdown of family relations, and seek support for measures to strengthen the capacity of families to cope with stress. The different organisations are not inert instruments of a conscious actor called 'government': by their presence and their expertise, they are 'framing' the question in a particular way. Having a housing corporation is an inducement to respond to the problem by building houses – 'when you've got a hammer in your hand, everything looks like a nail'.

What we are seeing here is the way in which organisations constitute problems by shaping and filtering the perceptions of members. Organisations themselves, through their structure and culture, determine:

- first, what counts as a problem that may require action to solve
- secondly, what values and preferences will be invoked in dealing with that problem.

In the case of draining the meadow, the problem was fairly straightforward: the farmers concerned agreed that there was a problem, and what had to be done to solve it. The difficulty lay in organising people to accomplish this. Yet problems are not necessarily recognised as such, and organisations shape the way individuals come to recognise them.

For example, while 'the problem' of HIV/AIDS had a real existence outside hospitals and laboratories, the way it was recognised and dealt with was strongly determined by the organisational framework within which it was being handled. Different kinds of scientists in a laboratory, doctors in a clinic, activists in the gay community, and people living with virus itself, all had a different approach, a different way of structuring the problem and what to do about it. The outcome was a result of the interaction between their skills, institutional position and resources they could deploy. The recognition of a problem itself depended on the existence of some group that could 'take it on board', i.e. that was able to accomodate it within its range of concerns. So we cannot see organisations as simply responding to pre-existing 'problems'.

Organisation as a Pattern of Organising

Even if we were content to regard organisations as instruments for the rational solution of known problems, we have seen that organisational action involves more than what happens inside any single organisation. The work of organisations brings them into contact with other organisations and individuals, and it can only be understood in relation to these 'significant others' which are 'outside' the organisation. The organisational process includes the way that the links among these various participants are constructed and maintained, so it has to be seen as a continuing pattern of organising rather than the operation of a pre-existing machine.

As we have seen, this has been noticed by researchers looking at organisation from several different perspectives. Political scientists looking at the policy process have labelled this inter-organisational pattern the 'issue network' or 'policy community'. Other researchers have found this knitting-together of different parts even within organisations as cohesive as the business firm, which has been described as a 'political coalition' or a 'network of treaties'. The recognition that this knitting-together has to take in participants from outside the organisation has given rise to the idea of 'stakeholders': that is, individuals or bodies who are part of the pattern of organising, even if they are not part of the organisation.

So we can see a pattern of organising which flows through and between formal organisations. In this perspective, we can see the organising which underlies the operation of (for instance) the workplace. The workplace is a venue for organising: the people involved have to create and maintain a stable pattern of working together. In doing this, they draw on the elements of our three models – authoritative rules, self-interested exchange, and affiliation – and each workplace does it in its particular way. In some workplaces there may be more reliance on authority (e.g. 'firm management'), in others, more on self-interest (e.g. 'incentive systems'), or on affiliation (e.g. 'team-building'), but there will be some of each element.

Shaping the Pattern

The question then becomes, 'what shapes this pattern of organising?' We have already seen that organisational structure has to be seen as the product of action – that structure informs action, and action reconstitutes structure – but how does this happen? What are (in Giddens's term) the 'structuring properties' of organisational action which lead it to be reproduced, and in this way to reconstitute organisational structure?

We can think of organisational action as being made up of three dimensions: their *framework of meaning*, the *institutional setting* and the *underlying values*. These are analytically distinct but in practice they interact closely with one another.

Figure 11.1: Dimensions of Organising

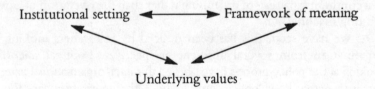

Institutional setting ←——→ Framework of meaning

Underlying values

The framework of meaning is the way that people make sense of the organisational activity: what action is appropriate, and why. There are different sources of meaning for organisational participants. They are likely to have some particular functional expertise: they know about surveying, for instance, or personnel, or marketing, and their training and experience in these fields will give each participant a perspective on what to do in the organisation. There are likely to be shared and distinctive understandings and patterns of action within the organisation: 'this is what we are concerned with here'. This means that when organisational activity crosses institutional boundaries there may be friction between these alternative understandings. In these cases the people concerned find that they have to develop a way of understanding and talking about the activity which they share with the other participants. If the surveyor, the personnel director and the marketing manager find themselves engaged in preparing the corporate plan for the next five years they will all have their own ideas about what is important but they have to find a common language (which may simply be money: $x for the survey branch, $y for personnel and $z for marketing).

Secondly, organisational activity takes place in a particular institutional setting – that is, in a known framework of bodies and offices, like 'Department of Roads', 'Chief Engineer', 'National Motorists' Association' or 'Product Coordinator'. The way these institutional forms are set up helps to shape the nature of the action that takes place there. If there is a Department of Roads and a Department of Railways, then each will tend to limit its concern with transport planning to the needs of the service for which it is responsible. If the government wants more broadly based planning for the transport system as a whole, it may decide to merge the two departments into a single Department of Transport. We can also see here the interaction between framework of meaning and institutional setting: the people with expertise about trains will be in the Department of Railways (and will be likely to resist the proposed amalgamation with Roads as a way of protecting their expertise).

Thirdly, organisational activity rests on an underlying pattern of values which inform both the frameworks of meaning people employ and the institutional settings within which they operate. A concern for 'development' will support specialised frameworks of meaning (e.g. about logging the forests, clearing the land, damming the rivers, etc) and also the institutional settings within which this knowledge is appropriately deployed (e.g. a Forestry Commission, a Land Settlement Agency, a Department of Water Resources, etc). A growing concern for the environment is likely to give rise to both a new framework of meaning and an institution in which it is used (e.g. an Environment Protection Authority).

The different dimensions of organising reinforce one another and produce different patterns of organisation. A Department of the Environment will be a different sort of organisation from a Department of Roads: even if they have the same constitutional basis they will rest on different values and mobilise different sorts of expertise. The Department of the Environment will also differ from the local environment protection group: it may share much of the underlying pattern of values, but the frameworks of meaning that it mobilises are likely to be more specialised, professional and comparative, and as a government department it has to relate the claims of the environment to all the other interests and values to which the government is committed.

The interplay of these dimensions of organising underlies our three models of organisation: we can now see how participants draw on these models to constitute organisation, and how they can draw on different models at the same time, but in varying combinations. In each model a particular way of valuing outcomes informs and reflects:

• the framework of meaning that participants apply to the problem
• the appropriate institutional setting for dealing with the question
• the validity of outcomes.

For instance, a state's youth unemployment is recognised as a major policy problem, and it is argued by some that the best way to combat it is to remove the statutory restraints on the employment of young people (e.g. minimum wages). This claim is hotly contested, and the conflict reflects the clash between the market and the hierarchical model.

The market model contains a framework of meaning which sees life as a set of self-interested exchanges between rational actors, an institutional setting in which these exchanges can take place (an informed market-place, with the policeman and the law of contract in the background), and a way of valuing the outcomes (essentially, seeing any agreement reached between a prospective employer and a young person as, by definition, fair and appropriate).

The hierarchical model rests on a different set of values, seeing the young person as not having the bargaining power (or, perhaps, the judgement) to preserve his/her best interests, and therefore needing the protection of a set of institutions (such as wage-fixing bodies) in which the relative claims of young people and employers can be weighed through the development of a way of thinking about the question: policies, guidelines, assumptions, ways of calculating, etc.

In other words, each model offers a distinct way of organising the employment of young people (and the community model offers a third way). The actual pattern of organising will contain elements of both. Few people advocate statutory wage provisions which take no account of market forces, or a totally free market in which there are no legal constraints on employers. But people may argue for change in the direction of one model or another – more reliance on lower wages, for instance (i.e. a shift towards the market model), or a call on all employers to employ one more young person in the public interest (i.e. mobilising the community model).

Organising and Change

When we view organisation as patterned action then the potential for change is always there. Yet it is often seen as difficult to accomplish. In the extensive debate on organisational change it is generally assumed that organisations should change, and that the evident difficulty in bringing about organisational change is a major problem. In one sense, it should not be surprising that organisations resist change: organisation is a way of stabilising action and generating predictability, so we should expect organisations to be resistant to change. On the other hand, if organisation is created and sustained by what people do, can't they simply change what they do, and in this way change the organisation?

It depends on which people we're talking about. Commonly, the people talking about the need for organisational change are in positions of power towards the top of the organisation: in the context of a literature (and a world of practice) which sees the manager as a heroic individual, it is seen as the manager's task to transform the organisation, and the worth of managers is measured by their ability to 'turn the organisation around'. They do not find this an easy thing to do, particularly when (as is often the case), they are relatively new to the job. As they see it, when they try to get things done differently, they meet with suspicion, hostility and resentment which is an obstacle to the achievement of the desired change. The workers themselves may argue that they are simply trying to do their jobs in the face of continual interference from managers who have no idea of the needs of the job. The workers don't see themselves as mindless automatons: they are accustomed to doing the task and being organised in a particular way, and they are likely to be unimpressed by demands that this be changed, particularly if they have had no part in framing this agenda of change.

Here, the debate about organisational change reflects the model of organisation on which people are drawing (perhaps unconsciously) in the debate. Again, the dominant model is that of bureaucracy, and the organisation is seen as a machine for the accomplishment of authorised goals. If the goals (or the mode of achieving them) are changed by those in authority, the organisation should follow the lead given. If it does not, it is seen as conservative, inert, and guilty of 'wilful obstruction' (as one frustrated reformer entitled his autobigraphy).

But as we have seen from our discussion of the dimensions of organising, the pattern of activity in organisation does not simply reflect authorised directions: it reflects the shared frameworks of meaning, and the institutional settings in which these are pursued. Changing the pattern of activity is likely to involve change to all of these.

The introduction of equal employment opportunity (EEO) in public employment offers a good example. Changes in the authorised directions – statements about procedures for recruitment and promotion, forms of advertisement and interview, provisions for training and promotion – did not in themselves bring about change. They reflected changes in the underlying values of public employment (e.g. what was understood by equity). They legitimated the changes to the framework of meaning in which public employment was conducted, and the new institutional settings (e.g. the emergence of executives responsible for EEO, and plans for its achievement). But these values had to be repeatedly enacted in particular cases of recruitment and promotion, and repeatedly defended against pressure to roll them back.

Change may not necessarily be an initiative of the authorised decision makers, but may be forced on them from outside. Organisations are constantly interacting with the world outside, and the organisational environment can be considered a source of change: organisations adjust to changes in their environment, keeping in step with their 'relevant others'. EEO is a demand for change within the organisation which has primarily come from outside it. But part of the change which this demand has produced is the installation of EEO staff within the organisation whose primary concern is to promote changes in organisational practice. And the principal resource of the EEO staff in pursuing these changes is the existence of pressure from outside. In the same way, other specialist staff in the organisation may have similar links with supervisory bodies concerned with industrial relations, air pollution, certification of standards, etc. In each case there may be both 'inside' and 'outside' pressures for change in organisational practice.

And if the 'outside' pressures find that they do not get a satisfactory response from inside the organisation, they may campaign for a different sort of organisation in which their concerns will be respected. Specialised interests, such as farmers or consumer groups or doctors, may demand a separate department within government devoted to their concerns, one which will be staffed by people who speak their language and with whom they can maintain discourse. So the very existence of the organisation may be a consequence of a demand for organisational change.

Changes in technology may also spur change in organisations. For instance, advances in computing may enable widespread decentralisation within an organisation. But by the same token, they may enable the centre to maintain even closer control over its branches. Technological change may lead to organisational change, and it can be argued that it is an independent force for change. But it can also be argued that the change comes not from the technological change but from the use which organisational participants make of it, in this case to extend or to reduce central control.

So, change in organisation is not simply the work of authorised decisionmakers. But to the extent that it is, they draw on the three models of organisation. Take, for instance, the task of achieving change in the workplace. The bureaucratic model sees the organisation as being governed by the decisions of the management: accordingly, change can be achieved by giving new and explicit directions: reorganisation, rationalisation, new procedures, corporate plans, training, etc.

The market model, by contrast, sees organised activity in terms of self-interested exchanges, which suggests that the way to change behaviour in the organisation is to give people incentives. Workplace reform could be approached through offering incentives such as 'productivity bonuses' for the workers, or 'performance pay' for the managers trying to achieve the reform. Workplace reform will come when enough people see it as being in their interest.

The community model, by contrast, sees organisation in terms of shared norms and a sense of belonging: this suggests pursuing organisational change through collective exercises in goal setting, and other forms of 'team building'. This model has its focus on the culture of the workplace, and aims to transform that culture.

These models of organisation offer distinct approaches to workplace change, but in practice attempts to achieve change in organisations will take in elements of all of them, though there may be a shift in favour of one rather than another. However, they may cut across one another: for instance, changing the pay system to give more pay to the most productive individuals may threaten the collective culture of the workplace, and lead to division and resentment in the workplace. Asking the workers themselves to devise the reform strategy would ensure that it would be firmly rooted in the culture of the workplace, but at the expense of managerial control. Again, there is no magic answer:

the organisational process embodies a number of potentially contradictory forces.

Organisation and the Individual

How does this analysis help the individual to make sense of the organisational world and to participate in it?

Perhaps the most important lesson to be learned has been the complexity of organised action. When we look at the specifics of the organisational arrangements that surround us we find that they are composed of inputs from different organisational players who do not necessarily share the same objectives or even the same interest in the subject. It becomes difficult to see policy questions as simple problems – things that 'they' should do something about. 'They' have dissolved into a range of players pursuing distinct agendas, into which any particular policy question has to be fitted.

We have seen, too, that organisation is not a pre-existing thing waiting to be wheeled into action, but a pattern of activity which the participants put together by drawing on known models of organising. They are likely to draw on all of the models, but in different combinations, leading to considerable scope for variation in the pattern of organisation.

For these reasons organisation is characterised by complexity and ambiguity. Participants and students tend to adopt 'working simplifications', e.g. when they say 'the problem is …' or 'the government wants …' or 'the operation of the housing market'. Yet they are aware that the nature of the problem depends on the assumptions made and the standpoint taken. They know that the government's wants are extremely muffled, and the organisational pattern relating to housing only loosely resembles the market model. This is not a problem as long as we are not trapped by the convenient simplifications, for instance by saying 'well, if it's a market, it should work like this …'. We have to remember that the situation on the ground remains an empirical question.

Applications

We have seen that 'organisation' refers not only to the activities *of* organisations, but also to the organising that goes on within and between them. Some of the most interesting questions about organisation tend to emerge in multi-organisational fields. There are four areas, in particular, where this analysis of 'organising' can usefully be applied.

The first is in relation to the organising of *government*. We have seen that a phrase like 'the machinery of government' is an enormous simplification: it is neither accurate nor very helpful. There is a wide range of organisations involved in government – not just parliament and the civil service, but also specialised agencies, professions, interest groups, local and regional governments, trade unions, etc. The critical question is how these relate to one another, and statements like 'ministers make the decisions and the civil service carries them out' or 'separate agencies of government are established to deal with separate, specialised concerns' are enormous simplifications. This has become particularly evident in recent years as the nature of the organised relationships in government – e.g. between politicians and officials, and between government and the public – has come under intense scrutiny and been subject to large and continuing changes. There is now a great interest in what has been labelled 'governance', i.e. how we organise things.

A second area where the importance of organising has become evident is in relation to *economic activity* – in particular, how is industry organised? The division between 'state' and 'economy', or 'private sector' and 'public sector' is another of these simplifications – sometimes helpful, sometimes not. There has been interest in the significance of government action in economic development, and whether or not there should be an 'industry policy' (or whether there already is one). The attention has shifted from 'what is the boundary between government and business?' to 'how is the whole show put together?', as researchers have tried to clarify the 'governance regime' in particular fields of economic activity.

Thirdly, the organising of the *workplace* has also come under intense scrutiny, and the efficiency and the social acceptability of large bureaucratic organisational forms has been questioned. There is great interest in smaller, more autonomous units, 'flatter structures' (i.e. less hierarchy), and the development of close, cooperative relations between self-managing structures. At the same time, there is concern to give individual managers more autonomy from central corporate controls, and to require them to produce visible results (e.g. performance indicators) which give them a particular interest in maintaining hierarchic control. And there has been increasing governmental concern in some aspects of the workplace, e.g. equal employment opportunity, or the adequacy of industrial training. So the organising of the workplace is

subject to many pressures for change, and they do not all push in the
same direction.

The fourth area of organising to which this approach can be applied
is *welfare*. Despite talk about the 'welfare state' it has become clear that
welfare is an area where state bodies, community organisations, businesses
and families all interact with one another. Social and economic change
has challenged the existing pattern of organising. For instance, as a greater
proportion of women take on full-time paid employment the organisation of child care has become problematic. It may be provided through
market, bureaucratic or community forms of organisation – most likely
a contested mixture of all three.

Review

1. The book has focused on the process of organising rather than result
   ('organisations').
2. Organisations are often seen as things that rational people create
   for their own purposes.
3. The 'social contract' refers to the idea that political organisations
   are the result of agreements between rational individuals.
4. 'Bounded rationality' refers to the idea that people's ability to
   collect, interpret and decide on the basis of information is limited.
5. Existing organisations shape what counts as a problem, and how
   it should be solved.
6. No organisation exists on its own: 'networks', 'treaties', 'stakeholders', 'coalitions' and 'teams' refer to inter-organisational
   relationships.
7. The resulting pattern of organisation is the result of the institutional
   setting, the framework of meaning, and the underlying values.
8. Change is a problem for the view of organisations as a pattern of
   (not necessarily rational) action.
9. Each model suggests a different view of change: as the result of
   pressure from the top, and resistance to it; as a result of incentives
   and constraints; and as dependent on organisational culture.
10. Organisation is complex and ambiguous, though to get by we adopt
    convenient simplifications.
11. Inter-organisational relationships are significant in understanding
    recent changes in government, industry policy, industrial relations
    and social welfare.

Questions for Discussion

1. In the organisations of which you are a member, can you identify and distinguish (i) the institutional setting (ii) the framework of meaning and (iii) the underlying values?
2. How and why are you committed to changing or conserving a particular organisation of which you are a member?
3. Which 'convenient simplifications' help maintain the organisation of the school or university/college of which you are a member?
4. How will what you have read in this book help you to change and conserve organisations to which you are committed?

Further Reading

The book has drawn on several overlapping fields of research and writing. Some are surveyed in the three more advanced texts recommended at the end of the introduction: Hood (1986); Harmon and Mayer (1986) and Marchment and Thompson, eds (1993).

The following books and articles are meant to provide students with signposts, a recent survey, a bibliography and a rough label for each field of research.

March and Olsen (1984 and 1989), North (1990), and Powell and DiMaggio (1991) on the 'new institutionalism'.

Kaufmann (1986) on 'mechanisms of coordination' or (in German) 'Ordnungstheorie'.

Atkinson and Coleman (1992) on 'policy networks'.

Friedland and Robertson (1990), and Campbell et al, eds (1991) on 'governance'.

Moe (1984 and 1991) and Hodgson (1988) on the 'economics of organisation'.

Mueller (1989) and McLean (1986) on 'public choice'.

Elster (1989), Weale (1990) and Monroe (1991) on 'rational choice'.

Alt and Shepsle (1990) on 'positive political economy'.

Ostrom, V. (1989) and Ostrom, E. (1990) on 'collective action'.

References

Alt, J. and Crystal, K., 1983. *Political Economics* Brighton: Wheatsheaf.

Alt, J. and Shepsle, K., eds 1990. *Perspectives on Positive Political Economy* Cambridge: Cambridge University Press.

Altman, D., 1988. 'Legitimation through Disaster: AIDS and the Gay Movement' in E. Fee and D. Fox, eds *AIDS: the Burdens of History* Berkeley: University of California Press pp. 301–315.

Altman, D., 1991. 'Community Organisations and the New Political Challenges' *National AIDS Bulletin* (Canberra), September, pp. 13–16.

Aoki, M., Gustafsson, B. and Williamson, O. E., 1990. *The Firm as a Nexus of Treaties* London: Sage.

Atkinson, M. and Coleman W., 1992. 'Policy Networks, Policy Communities and the Problems of Governance' *Governance* 5(2), pp. 154–80.

Baumol, W., 1982. 'Contestable Markets: An Uprising in the Theory of Industry Structure' *The American Economic Review* 72 (1), pp. 1–15.

Bayer, R., 1989. *Private Acts, Social Consequences: AIDS and the Politics of Public Health* New York: Macmillan.

Blinder, A., 1987. *Hard Heads and Soft Hearts* Reading, Mass: Addison Wesley.

Butler, R., 1983. 'Control through Markets, Hierarchies and Communes: A Transactional Approach to Organisational Analysis' in A. Francis, J. Turk and P. Willman, eds *Power Efficiency and Institutions: A Critical Appraisal of the 'Markets and Hierarchies' Paradigm* London: Heinemann, pp. 137–58.

Campbell, J., Hollingsworth, J. and Lindberg, L., eds, 1991. *Governance of the American Economy* Cambridge: Cambridge University Press.

Caton, C., 1990. *Homelessness in America* New York: Oxford University Press.

Cawson, A., 1986. *Corporatism and Political Theory* Oxford: Blackwell.

Clegg, S., 1989. *Frameworks of Power* London: Sage.

Clegg, S., 1990. *Modern Organizations* London:Sage.

Coase, R., 1960. 'The Problem of Social Cost' *Journal of Law and Economics* 3, pp. 1–44.

Coase, R., 1974. 'The Lighthouse in Economics' *Journal of Law and Economics* 17(2), pp. 357–76.

Colebatch, H. and Degeling, P., 1986. 'Talking and Doing in the Work of Administration' *Public Administration and Development* 6, pp. 339–56.

Crago, H., 1991. 'Homeless Youth: How the Solution Becomes Part of the Problem' *Quadrant,* September, pp. 26–31.

Crozier, M., 1963. *The Bureaucratic Phenomenon* Chicago: University of Chicago Press.

Dahl, R, 1961. *Who Governs* New Haven: Yale University Press.

Dahl, R., 1963. *Modern Political Analysis* Englewood Cliffs: Prentice Hall.

Deakin, N. and Wright, A., 1990. *Consuming Public Services* London and New York: Routledge and Kegan Paul.

Demsetz, H., 1968 'Why Regulate Utilities?' *Journal of Law and Economics* 11, pp. 55–66.

Denhardt, R., 1993. *The Pursuit of Significance: Strategies for Managerial Success in Public Organizations* Belmont, California: Wadsworth.

Donahue, J., 1989. *The Privatization Decision* New York: Basic Books.

Donaldson, L., 1985. *In Defence of Organisation Theory* Cambridge: Cambridge University Press.

Douglas, M., 1987. *How Institutions Think* London: Routledge and Kegan Paul.

Dunford, R., 1992. *Organisational Behaviour* Sydney: Addison Wesley.

Dunleavy, P., 1991. *Democracy, Bureaucracy and Public Choice: Economic Explanations in Political Science* Hertford: Wheatsheaf.

Dunsire, A., 1973. *Administration: the Word and the Science* London: Martin Robertson.

Elster, J., 1989. *Nuts and Bolts for the Social Sciences* Cambridge: Cambridge University Press.

Feldman, M. S. and March, J. G., 1981. 'Information as Signal and Symbol' *Administrative Science Quarterly* 26, pp. 17–86.

Francis, A., et al, eds 1983. *Power Efficiency and Institutions* London: Heinemann.

Friedland, R. and Robertson, A. F., 1990. *Beyond the Marketplace: Rethinking Economy and Society* New York: Aldine de Gruyter.

Friedman, M. and Friedman, R., 1980. *Free to Choose* San Diego: Harcourt Brace.

Garfinkel, H., 1967. *Studies in Ethnomethodology* New York: Prentice Hall.

Giddens, A., 1984. *The Constitution of Society* Cambridge: Polity.

Goodsell, C., 1986. *The Case for Bureaucracy: A Public Administration Polemic* Chatham, New Jersey: Chatham House.

Gretschmann, K., 1986. 'Solidarity and Markets' in F-X. Kaufmann, G. Majone and V. Ostrom, eds *Guidance Control and Evaluation in the Public Sector: the Bielefeld Interdisciplinary Project* Berlin and New York: De Gruyter, pp. 387–405.

Hamilton, G. and Biggart, N., 1988. 'Market, Culture and Authority: A Comparative Analysis of Management and Organisation in the Far East' *American Journal of Sociology* 94(Supplement), S52–S94.

Hardin, G., 1968. 'The Tragedy of the Commons' *Science* 162, 1243–48.

Harmon, M. and Mayer, R., 1986. *Organisation Theory For Public Administration* Boston: Little Brown.

Heclo, H. and Wildavsky, A., 1974. *The Private Government of Public Money* London: Macmillan.

Heclo, H., 1978. 'Issue Networks and the Executive Establishment' in A. King, ed *The American Political System* Washington: American Enterprise Institute.

Heilbroner, R. and Thurow, L., 1982. *Economics Explained* New Jersey: Prentice Hall.

Hilmer, F., 1989. *New Games, New Rules: Work in Competitive Enterprise* North Ryde: Angus and Robertson.

Hindess, B., 1989. *Political Choice and Social Structure: An Analysis of Action, Interests and Rationality* Aldershot, Hants: Edward Elgar.

Hirschmann, A., 1970. *Exit Voice and Loyalty* Cambridge, MA: Harvard University Press.

Hjern, B. and Porter, D., 1981. 'Implementation Structures: A New Unit of Administrative Analysis' *Organization Studies* 2, 211–24.

Hodgson, G., 1988. *Economics and Institutions* Cambridge: Polity.

Hood, C., 1976. *The Limits of Administration* London: Wiley.

Hood, C., 1986. *Administrative Analysis: An introduction to Enforcement and Organisations* Brighton: Wheatsheaf.

Hula, R., 1988. *Market-based Public Policy* Basingstoke: Macmillan in association with Policy Studies Organisation.

Hume, D., 1911. *A Treatise of Human Nature* London: Dent.

Institute of Medicine, 1988. *Homelessness, Health and Human Needs* Washington, DC: National Academy Press.

Jacques, E., 1991. 'In Praise of Hierarchy' in G. Thompson, J. Francis, R. Levacic and J. Mitchell, eds *Market Hierarchies and Networks: the Coordination of Social Life* London: Sage in association with the Open University Press, pp. 108–18.

Kaufmann, F-X., Majone, G. and Ostrom, V. eds 1986. *Guidance Control and Evaluation in the Public Sector* New York: De Gruyter.

Kinsey, A., Pomeroy, W. and Martin, C., 1948. *Sexual Behavior in the Human Male* Philadelphia: W.B. Saunders.

Kirp, D. and Bayer, R., eds 1992. *AIDS in the Industrialized Democracies: Passions, Politics and Policies* New Brunswick New Jersey: Rutgers University Press.

Krusselberg, H-G, 1986. 'Markets and Hierarchies' in F-X. Kaufmann, G. Majone and V. Ostrom, eds *Guidance Control and Evaluation in the Public Sector* Berlin and New York: De Gruyter, pp. 349–86.

Kuhnle, S. and Selle, P., 1992. *Government and Voluntary Organizations: A Relational Perspective* Aldershot: Avebury.

Lane, J-E., ed 1987. *Bureaucracy and Public Choice* London: Sage.

Larmour, P., 1990. 'Public Choice in Melanesia: Community, Bureaucracy and the Market in Land Management' *Public Administration and Development* 10, pp. 53–68.

Laver, M., 1981. *The Politics of Private Desires* Harmondsworth: Penguin.

Laver, M., 1983. *Invitation to Politics* Oxford: Martin Robertson.

Leblebici, H. et al, 1991. 'Institutional Change and the Transformation of Interorganizational Fields: An Organizational History of the US Broadcasting Industry' *Administrative Science Quarterly* 36, pp. 333–63.

Legge, K., 1984. *Evaluating Planned Organizational Change* London: Academic Press.

Lipsky, M., 1978. 'Standing the Study of Policy Implementation on its Head' in W. D. Burnham and M. W. Weinberg, eds *American Politics and Public Policy* Cambridge, Mass: Cambridge University Press, pp. 391–402.

Luce, D. and Raiffa, H., 1957. *Games and Decisions: Introduction and Critical Survey* New York: Wiley.

Lukes, S., 1974. *Power: A Radical View* London: Macmillan.

Mann, J., Tarantola, D. and Netter, T., eds 1992. *AIDS in the World: A Global Report* Cambridge, MA and London: Harvard University Press.

March, J. and Feldman, M., 1988. 'Information in Organizations as Signal and Symbol' in J. March, ed *Decisions and Organizations* Oxford: Basil Blackwell.

March, J. and Olsen, J., 1984. 'The New Institutionalism: Organizational Factors in Political Life' *American Political Science Review* 78(3), pp. 734–49.

March, J. and Olsen, J., 1989. *Rediscovering Institutions* New York: Free Press.

Marchment, R. and Thompson, G., eds 1993. *Managing the UK: An Introduction to its Political Economy and Public Policy* London: Sage.

McLean, I., 1986. *Public Choice: An Introduction* Oxford: Blackwell.

Mintzberg, H., 1973. *The Nature of Managerial Work* New York: Harper and Row.

Mintzberg, H., 1983. *Power In and Around Organisations* Englewood Cliffs: Prentice Hall.

Mitroff, I. I., 1983. *Stakeholders of the Organisational Mind* San Francisco: Jossey-Bass.

Moe, T., 1984. 'The New Economics of Organisation' *American Journal of Political Science* 28(4): pp. 739–777.

Moe, T., 1991. 'Politics and the Theory of Organisation' *Journal of Law Economics and Organisation* 7 (Special Issue), pp. 106–29.

Monroe, K., ed. 1991. *The Economic Approach to Politics* New York: Harper Collins.

Morgan, G., 1986. *Images of Organisation* Beverley Hills: Sage.

Mueller, D., 1989. *Public Choice II: a Revised Edition of Public Choice* Cambridge and New York: Cambridge University Press.

Nicholson, M., 1970. *Conflict Analysis* London: English Universities Press.

North, D., 1990. *Institutions, Institutional Change and Economic Performance* Cambridge: Cambridge University Press.

Olson, M., 1965. *The Logic of Collective Action* Cambridge, MA: Harvard University Press.

Oppenheimer, G., 1992. 'Causes, Cases and Cohorts: The Role of Epidemiology in the Historical Construction of AIDS' in E. Fee and D. Fox, eds *AIDS: the Making of a Chronic Disease* Berkeley: University of California Press, pp. 49–83.

Osborne, D. and Gaebler, T., 1993. *Reinventing Government: How the Entrepreneurial Spirit is Transforming the Public Sector* New York: Plume.

Ostrom, E., 1990. *Governing the Commons: the Evolution of Institutions of Collective Action* Cambridge: Cambridge University Press.

Ostrom, V., 1989. 'Some Developments in the Study of Market Choice, Public Choice, and Institutional Choice' in J. Rabin et al, eds *Handbook of Public Administration* New York and Basel: Marcel Dekker, pp. 861–82.

Ouchi, W., 1980. 'Markets, Bureaucracies and Clans' *Administrative Science Quarterly* 25(1), pp. 129–41.

Padgug, R. and Oppenheimer, G., 1992. 'Riding the Tiger: AIDS and the Gay Community' in E. Fee and D. Fox, eds *AIDS: the Making of a Chronic Disease* Berkeley: University of California Press, pp. 245–78.

Patton, C., 1990. *Inventing AIDS* New York and London: Routledge.

Peters, T., 1992. *Liberation Management* London: Macmillan.

Pettitt, P., 1985. 'The Prisoner's Dilemma and Social Theory: An Overview of Some Issues' *Politics*, 20(1), pp. 1–11.

Pfeffer, J., 1982. *Organizations and Organization Theory* Marshfield, Mass: Pitman Press.

Pfeffer, J., 1982. *Organisations and Organisation Theory* Pitman: Boston.

Powell, W. W. and DiMaggio, P., 1991. *The New Institutionalism and Organisational Analysis* Chicago: University of Chicago Press.

Pressman, J. and Wildavsky, A., 1984. *Implementation* Berkeley: University of California Press, third edition.

Ricketts, M., 1987. *The Economics of Business Enterprises* Brighton: Wheatsheaf.

Rigby, T. H., 1964. 'Traditional, Market and Organisational Societites and the USSR' *World Politics* 16(4), pp. 539–57.

Rigby, T. H., 1990. *The Changing Soviet System: Mono-organisational Socialism from its Origins to Gorbachev's Restructuring* London: Edward Elgar.

Schotter, A., 1985. *Free Market Economics: A Critical Appraisal* New York: St Martin's Press.

Scott, J., 1990. *Domination and the Arts of Resistance: Hidden Transcripts* New Haven and London: Yale University Press.

Sears, A., 1992. '"To Teach them how to Live" the Politics of Public Health from Tuberculosis to AIDS' *Journal of Historical Sociology* 5(1), pp. 61–83.

Self, P., 1977. *Administrative Theories and Politics* (second edition) London: Allen and Unwin.

Simon, H., 1976. *Administrative Behavior* (third edition) New York: Free Press.

Skocpol, T., 1985. 'Bringing the State Back In: Strategies of Analysis in Current Research' in P. Evans, D. Rueschemeyer and T. Skocpol, eds *Bringing the State Back In* Cambridge and New York: Cambridge University Press.

Smith, A., 1974. *The Wealth of Nations* Books I–III Harmondsworth: Penguin.

Sontag, S., 1989. *AIDS and its Metaphors* London: Penguin.

Streeck, W. and Schmitter, P. C., eds 1985. *Private Interest Government: Beyond Market and State* London: Sage.

Streeck, W. and Schmitter, P., 1985. *Private Interest Government: Beyond Market and State* (Sage Studies in Neo-Corporatism) London, Beverley Hills and New Delhi: Sage.

Taylor, M., 1982. *Community, Anarchy and Liberty* Cambridge: Cambridge University Press.

Taylor, M., 1987. *The Possibility of Cooperation* Cambridge: Cambridge University Press.

Thompson, G., Frances, J., Levacic, R. and Mitchell, J., eds 1991. *Markets, Hierarchies and Networks: The Coordination of Social Life* London: Sage in association with the Open University.

Tönnies, F., 1957. *Community and Society* (Gemeinschaft and Gesellschaft, trans. C. Loomis) East Lansing: Michigan State University Press.

Uhr, J., ed 1991. *Program Evaluation* Canberra: Australian National University.

Veljanovski, C., ed 1989. *Freedom in Broadcasting* London: Institute of Economic Affairs.

Watney, S., 1987. *Policing Desire* London: Methuen.

Weale, A., 1990. 'Rational Choice and Political Analysis' in A. Leftwich, ed *New Developments in Political Science* Aldershot, Hants: Gower, pp. 196–211.

Weber, M., 1947. *The Theory of Social and Economic Organization* New York: Free Press.

Weber, M., 1991. 'Legal Authority in a Bureaucracy' in G. Thompson et al, eds *Markets, Hierarchies and Networks: The Coordination of Social Life* London: Sage in association with the Open University, pp. 119–27.

Weick, K., 1979. *The Social Psychology of Organising* (Second edition) Reading, Mass.: Addison Wesley.

Williamson, O., 1985. *The Economic Institutions of Capitalism* New York: Free Press.

Williamson, O. E. and Ouchi, W. G., 1983. 'The Markets and Hierarchies Programme of Research: Origins, Implications and Prospects' in A. Francis, J. Turk and P. Willman, eds *Power Efficiency and Institutions: A Critical Appraisal of the 'Markets and Hierarchies' Paradigm* London: Heinemann, pp. 13–33.

Williamson, O., 1975. *Markets and Hierarchies: Analysis and Antitrust Implications, A Study in the Economics of Internal Organisation* London and New York: Collier Macmillan and Free Press.

Wolf, C., 1987. 'Market and Non-Market Failures: Comparison and Assessment' *Journal of Public Policy* 7 (1), pp. 43–70.

Zagare, F., 1984. *Game Theory Concepts and Applications* Sage University Paper No. 44, Beverley Hills: Sage.

Glossary

Administration. The activity of organising, usually on behalf of other people. Administration is sometimes distinguished from 'management' as being concerned with organising things than people. See Dunsire (1973).

Collective Action. A phrase used to refer to the issues that arise from the interaction of rationally acting individuals, for example free riding, public goods and the 'tragedy of the commons'. See Laver (1981: 39–72) and Taylor (1987: 1–33).

Compliance. The tendency of people to follow rules, which may depend on whether they know the rule exists, whether they approve of it, and how easy it is to get away with avoiding it. See Hood (1986: 48–86).

Corporatism. A form of political organisation in which organised interests become part of the structure of government, representing the interests of their members and enforcing policy on them. See Cawson (1986: 58).

Externality. The effects of a deal on those not involved in making it. For example, the decision to build a polluting power plant may have 'external' effects on those living nearby. Externalities may be positive as well as negative, for example on the small businesses that depend on the wages of the employees of the polluting power plant. Government regulations may limit externalities, while taxes or subsidies may be used to 'internalise' them. For example, the external effects of a noisy party may be reduced by regulations on noise late at night, or by taxing parties (which may induce the party givers to hire a hall instead) or by bribing the neighbours (to compensate for their loss of sleep).

Free rider. A person who uses a good or service without paying for it (for example riding a bus or watching a football match). Some goods and services are more vulnerable to free riding than others, depending in part on the costs and technology of excluding non-payers.

Functional specialisation. Organising on the basis of specialised tasks. The specialist units may be whole organisations, e.g. Department of Roads, Department of Motor Transport, Department of Railways, or they may be components of one organisation, e.g. operations, personnel, marketing, corporate strategy, etc. Most forms of work involve functional specialisation; the question is how much this determines the structure of the organisation.

Goal displacement. The tendency for organisations to drift away from their original goals towards others, including self-preservation.

Goals. Organisations are often described as groups of people who come together to achieve goals that none of them could achieve individually. The perception that organisations exist in order to achieve goals is widely shared among people running organisations, though the belief that people in organisations do share goals is open to question.

Ideal type. A form of analysis that identifies a limited number of typical characteristics underlying a wide range of real examples. For example, Max Weber's 'ideal type' of bureaucracy consists of a list of characteristics found in varying degree in real organisations. But no single organisation will have all these characteristics.

Institution. A relatively persistent set of rules and expectations, normally treated as given, which provide moral and intellectual shape to organisations. Examples would include 'the crown' in Westminster systems of government, 'the constitution' in the USA, and 'gender' in most societies. See North (1990: 3–10), March and Olsen (1989: 1–19), and Powell and DiMaggio (1991: 1–38).

Invisible hand. The way order emerges out of many separate, and apparently uncoordinated activities. The phrase was first used by the political economist Adam Smith to describe the workings of a market economy, in which large-scale order was based on many small-scale decisions to buy and sell. By looking after their own interests (he argued), buyers and sellers in a market economy inadvertently look after the interests of everyone. By contrast, a 'visible hand' would deliberately direct production and distribution from a central agency, like a Ministry of Planning. Darwin's theory of evolution is another example of an 'invisible hand' theory. See Elster (1989; 96–7).

Management. 'Management' is one way of labelling the work of organising usually from the perspective of senior people in a hierarchy.

Like 'administration', the term is also applied to the people who are engaged in this work. See Mintzberg (1973).

Market failure. The absence of one or more of the conditions of a freely competitive market. For example, the presence of externalities violates the condition that deals should only affect those directly involved, while the existence of natural monopolies violates the condition that there should be a large number of sellers. The existence of market failures is used as a justification for government intervention to correct them. See Heilbroner and Thurow (1982: 157–78).

Model. A simplified picture of reality designed to draw attention to important variables and the relationships between them. For example, the weather is extremely complex but may be modelled as an interaction between (say) the temperature of the ocean, wind direction, and the amount of cloud cover. Models can, of course, mislead as well as predict.

Monopoly. Where there is only one supplier of a good or service, who can then control its price. Governments can create artificial monopolies by licensing only one supplier. But some goods and services are so-called 'natural monopolies', without government help. Examples are water and electricity supply, where there tends to be only one, or several, suppliers. Natural monopolies tend to emerge where there are networks, start-up costs are high, and the cost of adding one additional unit of service is low. These allow existing suppliers to drive off new entrants by cutting prices while they try to establish themselves.

Organisation. This term refers to people acting collectively: both to the way they act ('not enough organisation in this club') and to the pattern that emerges (i.e. referring to the club itself as an organisation). Usually, the term is used in the second sense; in this book we point out that having 'an organisation' is a consequence of people acting in a particular way, and we consider how this comes about.

Privatisation. The transfer of responsibility for a service, or its provision, from government to private companies, voluntary organisations, or individuals themselves (for example by contracting out, or selling government assets). It may include deregulation, though the sale of assets as a monopoly (for example water or telecommunications) may involve greater regulation of prices and quality. See Donahue (1989).

Public choice. The application of the assumptions of economics (particularly the rational individual) to the study of politics. See Mueller (1989) and McLean (1986).

Public goods. Goods that the private sector will not provide, because it cannot easily charge for them (and hence which tend to be provided by governments, funded from taxation, or not at all). The usual examples include defence, clean air and street lighting. Technically they are indivisible (if one person benefits, then everyone benefits) and non-excludable (those that have not paid can still benefit). In practice, excludability is often a matter of the price and availability of technology, for example by charging for the use of roads by toll gates or electronic meters. And private firms may provide the service on contract to government. 'Public goods', in this sense should not be confused with 'goods that benefit the public' (which, like food, are privately provided), or goods provided by the government (which, like schools, are excludable). See p. 33 and also Coase (1974) on whether or not lighthouses are public goods.

Rationality. Self-interested choice based on the outcomes of alternative actions. A person acts 'rationally' if, faced with a choice, she weighs up the alternatives according to their outcomes, and chooses the one that best achieves what she wants. Modern economics is based to the assumption that people behave in this way. In practice, choices are sometimes not available, or unclear, and people may choose for other reasons. See Monroe, ed (1991: 1–31).

Reciprocity. The assumption that if I help you, then you (or someone else) will help me in future. See Taylor (1982: 28–30).

Satisficing. A term invented by Herbert Simon to describe limits to rationality as it applied to people in organisations. Rationality assumed that people maximised something: their own self-interest, goals, or pay (in economic jargon). In practice, people had limited mental skills, limited commitments to the organisation's goals, and limited knowledge. Hence they 'satisficed' – did what was regarded as sufficient – rather than 'maximised'. See Simon (1976: 38–41, 240–44).

Selective benefits. A term invented by Mancur Olson to describe benefits that are only available to members of a group (for example cheap holidays for trade union members). Groups providing indivisible benefits to members and non-members may otherwise fail, through free riding. See Olson (1965).

Stakeholders. Individuals and groups within and outside an organisation that have an interest ('stake') in its activities (usually a wider group than those formally or constitutionally responsible). Thus stakeholders in a government department might include its clients, suppliers, employees, and other departments, as well as the minister to which it is formally responsible.

State. A loosely connected set of organisations claiming exclusive control over a particular territory and population. See (Skocpol 1985: 7). The state can be distinguished from 'the government', which is a group of senior officials who try to give state action coherence and direction.

Structure. This term is used to refer to what is seen as a relatively fixed element of organisation, a framework within which the action takes place. But it needs to be remembered that this is simply a stable and predictable way of acting, and that it is 'fixed' mainly in the knowledge and expectations of the people in the action. See Colebatch and Degeling (1986).

Tragedy of the commons. An image of environmental catastrophe devised by Garret Hardin. It shows how the pursuit of individual self-interest may, paradoxically, make everyone worse off. See Hardin (1968) and Ostrom (1990: 2–3).

Transaction costs. The costs of making and securing agreements. For example buying a house involves legal fees, title searches and so on in addition to the sale price. The costs of maintaining a system of titles, and courts to defend them, may also be included. Williamson (1975) explained the existence of hierarchically organised firms in terms of transaction costs. Firms could, in principle, subcontract the work they did, but if the costs of making and securing contracts became too high it would be cheaper to do the work 'in house'. See Ricketts (1987: 22–43) and Hodgson (1988: 195–216).

Index